OKAVANGO

Africa's Wetland Wilderness

To my parents,
for everything

OKAVANGO
Africa's Wetland Wilderness

Struik Publishers (Pty) Ltd
(a member of the Struik Publishing Group (Pty) Ltd)
Cornelis Struik House
80 McKenzie Street
Cape Town 8001

Reg No.: 54/00965/07

First published 1998

ISBN 1 86872 041 1

Project manager: Pippa Parker
Editor: Jenny Barrett
Designer: Dean Pollard
Illustrator: Annette Busse

Reproduction by Hirt & Carter (Pty) Ltd, Cape Town
Printed and bound by Tien Wah Press (Pte) Ltd, Singapore

Front cover: Black egret fishing

Spine: Floodplains of the Panhandle from the air

Back cover: Red lechwe (top); hippos at a water hole (2nd); juvenile lions fighting (3rd); sacred ibis (4th); leopard (5th); elephant herd drinking (bottom)

Endpapers: Papyrus stands in the Panhandle

Half title page: Elephant herd

Title page: Juvenile African jacana

Preface: Panhandle from the air

Contents page: African skimmer fishing

Pages 8–9: Kalahari dust storm; Popa Falls

Pages 16–17: Okavango Delta from the air; day waterlily

Pages 46–47: Hippo courtship ritual; African buffalo

Pages 76–77: Cattle egrets; giraffe drinking

Pages 164–165: Fishermen in the Panhandle; goat herd

ACKNOWLEDGEMENTS

My thanks go to the following people who so willingly volunteered their advice, assistance, support, knowledge, accommodation, transport, food, cold beers or friendship (and in many cases all of the above):

Rowland and Shirley-Ann Bailey, Megan Bailey, Colin Bell, David Bristow, Val Brown, Wolfgang Bürre and Moremi Safaris, Ian Clark, Deon and Crystal Cuyler, Jill and Perry Davies, Jan and Eileen Drotsky, Derek Flatt, Bob and Flo Fluxman, Jonathan Gibson and the directors of Afroventures, David Hartley, Wayne and Vanessa Hinde, Andre and Rosalind Joubert, Brian and Elaine Keene-Young, Leigh Kemp, Graeme Labe and Gametrackers Botswana, Ryan and Joanne Maritz, Witness Masasa, Prof. Spike McArthy and the Okavango Reasearch Group, Samantha McGrath, Tico McNutt, Peter Perlstein, Geoff and Nookie Randall, Veronica Roodt, Mark and Gilly Schwitter, Louis and Belinda Strauss, Marc Van Mourik and Murray Weiner. In addition, I am grateful to the many guides, drivers, boat drivers, polers and pilots who conveyed us safely over thousands of kilometres across the length and breadth of the Okavango Delta and all the staff of the lodges who offered us temporary relief from camping.

Thanks go to the Office of the President of Botswana for granting me permission to undertake this project and the Department of Wildlife and National Parks for allowing me the privilege of working in Moremi Game Reserve.

I also wish to thank the staff at Struik Publishers responsible for the production of this book, in particular Pippa Parker, Jenny Barrett, Dean Pollard and Peter Joyce.

And finally, thanks to Robyn, who was always there. Her love, assistance and, most importantly, her spectacular spotting have contributed immeasurably to this book.

Adrian Bailey
Cape Town
October 1997

The scene was mostly lush and verdant as I looked out from the river banks at Shakawe, on the edge of the Panhandle floodplain, one day in May 1995. Elegant papyrus fronds on the opposite bank were reflected in the calm waters of the Okavango River, and the deep blues and greens of the natural setting were punctuated by splashes of brilliant red as carmine bee-eaters hawked insects close to the water's surface. I had just emerged from a long stay in the Kalahari and Etosha, places which at the time were in the throes of a long drought.

Five days later I had 'done' the Okavango: I'd watched the Panhandle's innumerable birds, dumbstruck; I'd flown low over a myriad small islands, and landed successfully on an impossibly short dirt airstrip in the inner Delta; I'd walked for miles with a barefoot, unarmed guide, tracking hour-old lion spoor on Chief's Island; and I'd caught a glimpse of paradise in Moremi Game Reserve. I longed to stay, but apart from a few days snatched in between, it was not until July 1996 that I was able to return – and stay for more than a year.

To capture the Okavango's constantly fluctuating enigma in just a few pages is a daunting task. The place is so vast and wild, and so inaccessible, that it would take a decade just to explore it in its entirety. There is, however, a *genius loci*, or 'spirit of place', that pervades the region, and I hope that it suffuses these pages.

Okavango: Africa's Wetland Wilderness is structured using the metaphor of the theatre. The 'Prologue' presents the geological origins and human history of this unique area, and sets the scene for a discussion of the various habitats or landscapes in 'The Stage'. The most representative of the many creatures that live here are showcased in 'The Cast', while 'The Performance' focuses on the daily wildlife interactions which are an integral part of this wilderness arena. Lastly, the 'Epilogue' takes a look at the dangers that this vulnerable region and its occupants face. The photographs offer an unashamedly subjective view of the Okavango, and will no doubt illustrate some parts of the Delta better than others.

The book reflects about ten months of field time during 1996 and 1997. The time was spent living mostly in a tent, in some immaculate wilderness areas, in private concessions and in the Moremi Game Reserve. For a whole month at one stage, in treacherous wet-season conditions in Moremi, we encountered only one other vehicle. At times, herds of snorting buffalo interrupted our sleep. In one dry area elephant regularly visited to drink from a minute birdbath at the derelict camp where we lived, and lion often left their body prints on our doorstep before vanishing silently into the night.

The Okavango Delta is part of a much larger reality in Botswana, though, and is undergoing rapid change. Wilderness areas are under pressure throughout Africa, and the Okavango is no exception; indeed, the fact that it is still possible to have such intimate wildlife experiences as ours is remarkable. Sadly, land and other resources are at a premium, and the Okavango is truly fortunate to have persisted longer than most other wilderness areas. As well as revealing this unparalleled southern African setting, this book highlights some of the threats that challenge its continued existence.

Contents

Prologue

The making of
the Okavango

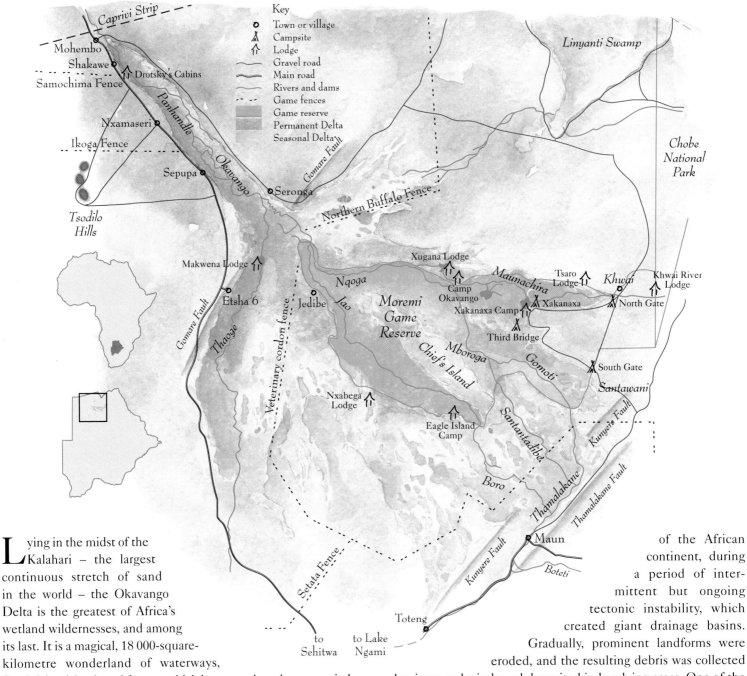

Key
- ⊙ Town or village
- ⚑ Campsite
- ⌂ Lodge
- Gravel road
- Main road
- Rivers and dams
- Game fences
- Game reserve
- Permanent Delta
- Seasonal Delta

Caprivi Strip

Mohembo
Shakawe
Samochima Fence
Drotsky's Cabins

Panhandle

Nxamaseri

Ikoga Fence

Linyanti Swamp

Okavango

Gomare Fault

Chobe National Park

Sepupa

Seronga

Northern Buffalo Fence

Tsodilo Hills

Gomare Fault

Makwena Lodge

Nqoga

Iao

Xugana Lodge

Maunachira

Tsaro Lodge

Khwai

Khwai River Lodge

Camp Okavango

Etsha 6

Jedibe

Thaoge

Moremi Game Reserve

Xakanaxa

Xakanaxa Camp

North Gate

Veterinary cordon fence

Third Bridge

Chief's Island

Mboroga

Gomoti

South Gate

Santawani

Nxabega Lodge

Santantadiba

Eagle Island Camp

Santantadiba

Kunyere Fault

Boro

Thamalakane

Thamalakane Fault

Setata Fence

Maun

Kunyere Fault

Boteti

to Sehitwa

to Lake Ngami

Toteng

Lying in the midst of the Kalahari – the largest continuous stretch of sand in the world – the Okavango Delta is the greatest of Africa's wetland wildernesses, and among its last. It is a magical, 18 000-square-kilometre wonderland of waterways, floodplains, islands and forests, which between them host a myriad animal and bird species. It also embraces a rich tapestry of human cultures.

There is much speculation about when and how the Delta was formed. What is certain, though, is that its development spanned millions of years, and was closely interwoven with the creation of its neighbour and host, the Kalahari, and of a succession of massive water systems that covered the region.

About 135 million years ago Gondwanaland, a colossal landmass which once comprised the combined bulk of today's southern hemisphere continents, began to fragment. India and Madagascar, Australia and Antarctica, and finally South America slowly split off and moved across the oceans, until by 100 million years ago the present configuration of landmasses had formed. Along with this separation went the lifting of the southern edges of the African continent, during a period of intermittent but ongoing tectonic instability, which created giant drainage basins. Gradually, prominent landforms were eroded, and the resulting debris was collected by rivers and winds and deposited in low-lying areas. One of the great continental depressions thus filled was the Kalahari basin.

The highest region in this basin is the Benguela plateau in Angola where, four or five million years ago, the run-off from rainfall began to ooze through the black, peaty turf to form the Cubango River. In a series of trickles and streams, the water gained momentum down the steep gradient before entering the savanna. The infant Cubango River – or Okavango, as it is known further downstream – was joined first by the Cuito and Chobe rivers from sources in the Angolan highlands, and then by the Upper Zambezi which began its journey in northwestern Zambia. All added to its volume as it flowed southeastwards. Passing through the exposed sands of the Kalahari, 400 kilometres from its source, it joined the Orange River and flowed westwards before spilling into the Atlantic Ocean.

Above: *A violent sandstorm rages over the southern Kalahari. Such storms were instrumental in shaping this arid region.* Right: *The northeastern edge of Sowa Pan is the only part of the once massive Lake Makgadikgadi which still holds water on a regular basis.*

About three million years ago geological instability caused the great river's flow to be diverted to the east. Still ploughing through the endless Kalahari sands, it now joined up with the Limpopo and found its way to the Indian Ocean. Later, when a warping of the earth's crust dammed back the giant river, the vast Lake Makgadikgadi formed in what is now northeastern Botswana. Though the lake survived successive humid and arid periods, its waters began to find alternative routes to the sea when further movements of the earth's crust tilted the subcontinent again.

The formation of the parallel Thamalakane, Kunyere and Gomare faults created an extension of the great East African Rift System, a series of loosely connected valleys that extends for 6 400 kilometres down the African continent, and the sinking of a section of the earth's crust between these fault lines created a trough that interrupted the flow of the Okavango River. Slowly this trough filled with the sediment discharged by the river and, in more arid times, by wind-blown debris, the accumulated material slowly forming a gently sloping fan. As the river flowed into this fan and deposited more sediment, channels became blocked and altered their course, and evaporation sapped what little momentum the river had. With progressively less water flowing from the Okavango River, Lake Makgadikgadi gradually dried up. The inland delta persisted though, and vegetation began to

Above: *The dry bed of the Boteti River. Before the formation of the Delta the river carried water from the Okavango River to Lake Makgadikgadi. Until recently it flowed regularly, but now its flow has all but ceased.* Opposite: *One of the many subsistence farms scattered across the Okavango's western edge.*

take root. The end result was a confusion of meandering, papyrus-lined channels, forested islands and lagoons – the Okavango Delta as we know it today. At times the Delta filled, its waters damming up against the Thamalakane Fault before flowing southeastwards through a break in the fault as the Boteti River, or southwards to form Lake Ngami. These areas were later to become focal points of human settlement, and though both the Boteti River and Lake Ngami are now dry, the river's west bank and the northern shores of the lake are still extensively populated.

All kinds of animals were drawn from the surrounding Kalahari thirstlands to the wealth of sustenance offered by the Delta. The evening air filled with the sounds of wildebeest, hartebeest and zebra herds coming to the waters to drink; reedbeds shook as multitudes of sitatunga and lechwe, both specialised semi-aquatic antelope, moved through the swamps. These animals drew predators – prides of lion and packs of wild dog – in their wake; at night, leopard slipped stealthily through the riverine forests. Crocodile lurked in the cool waters, and prolific fish and insect populations attracted vast flocks of migrant waterbirds.

It was to this setting that the region's first human occupants came. Early and Middle Stone Age humans appear to have inhabited the periphery of the Delta more than 100 000 years ago. The first of the Okavango Delta's modern-day inhabitants to arrive, however, were the San or Bushmen (known locally as the Basarwa). Most were hunter-gatherers, but some of these original settlers, a group called the Banoka (or river Bushmen), chose to live along the region's waterways, where they turned to

fishing for their livelihood. Originally confined to the southern edge of the Delta, the Boteti River and Lake Xau, they gradually spread through the region, following the channels on foot. They constructed reed rafts for fishing in the lagoons, but these craft were not suitable for actually travelling across the water, and it was not until later immigrants brought ferrous technology to the Delta that the Banoka began to use the region's now-traditional dugout canoe, the *mokoro*.

The first migration wave of modern Bantu-speaking people into the Delta region occurred roughly 250 years ago, and marked the start of a series of movements by various groups in the region. Since then, the salient feature of Botswana's population has been its fluidity: communities fragmented and amalgamated over the years, breaking away or moving on when pressures from within the tribe or from other, stronger groups became too great, and poorer groups at times became absorbed into richer communities, some making their own cultural or linguistic mark on their host societies. The result, today, is a country that has managed to strike a balance between national unity and retaining the distinctiveness of the various cultural groups.

It was the expansion of the Balozi tribe, inhabitants of a region some distance to the north of the Delta, during the mid-eighteenth century that started this chain of events, and led to the arrival of the first farmers in the Okavango Delta. The Hambukushu, who were living along the Zambezi River at the time, refused to pay tribute to the Balozi king, and they left the area to settle near Linyanti (in the extreme north of modern-day

Botswana), where they in turn displaced the Bayei people. The Bayei then travelled west along the waterways until they came to the edge of the Delta, an environment that was very similar to the one they had fled, and they soon spread through the newly found land. Primarily fishermen, they settled around Lake Ngami and the southern parts of the Delta, where the relatively open, shallow waters were suitable for trap-fishing. They also learnt to utilise the Delta's bounty in other ways, gathering riverine plants during the flood, tilling the floodplains when the waters receded, and hunting hippo. Here, too, they came across the area's long-established inhabitants, the Banoka. As the two groups did not compete for the same resources they were able to live side by side in harmony, and to exchange hunting, fishing and transport techniques.

In the meantime, despite having resettled, the Hambukushu in the Chobe area came under further pressure from the Balozi and they once again moved west. Chiefly agriculturalists, they settled for a short time on the Okavango River in the Caprivi region, but the majority of them fled yet again – this time from the threat of Portuguese slave traders – and finally settled in the northern parts of the Delta. Here they could farm the fertile floodplains in peace, and free from the scourge of the tsetse fly.

The arrival of the Batawana, in the later eighteenth century, was to have a powerful impact on the political and social fabric of the Delta region. The tribe had its origins in a group of people that broke away from the cattle-herding Bangwato of the eastern Kalahari and, in about 1800, made their way westwards under their leader Tawana. In due course they entrenched themselves around Toteng, near Lake Ngami. Once settled, they themselves became expansionist, eventually extending their authority and their culture across the entire Delta area. They also exacted tribute, in the form of meat and hunting trophies, from the other residents of the Delta area, and by 1850, it is thought, they owned most of the region's cattle. Today the Batawana, together with some dozen other groups that migrated to and across the Kalahari, are part of Tswana society, to which the great majority of Botswana's people belong and which is also prominent in the human geography of South Africa's northern areas. The Bangwato, however, remain the largest of Botswana's tribal components, accounting for about a quarter of Botswana's population.

The first European explorers arrived in the Okavango region in the mid-nineteenth century. Lured by legends of a great inland lake across the desert, David Livingstone, the renowned Scottish missionary and explorer, arrived on the shores of Lake Ngami in 1849. Here on the Delta's southern edge, the local people told him the water came from 'a country full of rivers, so many that no one can tell their number'.

Rumours of abundant wildlife and of kraals made of ivory soon spread. With the arrival of the European hunters and traders who followed eagerly in Livingstone's wake, both resident and newcomer became keenly aware of the commercial possibilities of the region's relatively unexploited wildlife. The subsistence use of wildlife was replaced by hunting for profit, and firearms flooded the area. Some Batawana themselves took up commercial hunting, and also pressured subordinate groups into obtaining trophies for them to trade. By 1867, the tusks of more than 10 000 elephant had passed through one trading post on the edge of the Kalahari, and within a couple of decades commercial exploitation had taken a noticeable toll on the region's game.

In 1883 a raiding party of pillaging Ndebele, from present-day Zimbabwe, launched a successful attack on the Batawana settlement at Toteng, netting large numbers of cattle and slaves. Two years later they attempted a repeat performance, but this time, the Batawana used their intimate knowledge of the Delta to good effect and retreated with their cattle to its many islands. More serious was the threat of disease: in 1894, both the wildlife and the Batawana cattle were decimated by rinderpest, an event that was to have far-reaching consequences. The thinning out of the herds led to the virtual elimination of the tsetse fly (which depends on blood for survival), and cattle-owners were able to move into previously infected areas. In time the wild herds recovered, tsetse fly re-established itself throughout the region,

and once again the people and their cattle were driven back to the Delta's periphery. Thus, despite the considerable human influx into parts of the Okavango over the years, most of the region remained uninhabitable: tsetse fly, along with malaria and the annual floods, confined livestock farmers to a 20-kilometre-wide belt around the Delta. Although the tsetse fly probably prevented a slide towards ecological disaster, competition between Botswana's cattle interests and those of the wildlife remains of profound concern to conservationists.

The turn of the century saw the arrival of the most colourful, and recognisable, of the Delta's modern inhabitants. The Mbanderu, a section of the Herero people, fled an accumulation of threats in their native Namibia (initially from the bloody confrontations of the Nama wars and then from German conquests), leaving behind the cattle on which their culture rested and their livelihood depended. At first these impoverished immigrants worked in servitude to the Batawana, but gradually they managed to rebuild their herds and regain a large measure of economic independence. Today they are among the more successful cattle farmers in Ngamiland, the district in which the Okavango falls. Mbanderu women are to this day easily identified by their long, colourful dresses, whose Victorian style is derived from the fashions favoured by the wives of Namibia's early European missionaries.

In 1915 the Batawana moved their capital to the base of the Delta, near what was to become Maun. Under their influence an

increasingly homogeneous society has emerged in Ngamiland and, except for the colourful Mbanderu, it is today difficult for the casual observer to tell the various tribal groupings from each other.

For much of the twentieth century Ngamiland was little more than a far-flung corner of the British Protectorate of Bechuanaland. In 1966 Botswana gained independence, and just a few years later, after the discovery of one of the world's largest diamond deposits, the country began to develop rapidly. The potential of the untouched northern wildernesses did not go unnoticed and the Okavango was soon caught up, albeit slowly at first, in the country's economic expansion. Safari and hunting operators moved in, though the expansion of this industry was initially checked by both the infestations of tsetse fly and mosquitoes and the inaccessibility of the area. Over the last few decades these barriers to 'progress' have been removed, and today tourism and related industries employ by far the majority of Ngamiland's workforce.

Commercialisation has brought its material rewards, but the bounty of the Okavango Delta is not unlimited and, as always, development creates a great many dangers. These dangers provide the focus of the Epilogue (pages 164–171).

Left: *Rra X Dudu, a Hambukushu farmer, at his village not far from Qhaaxhwa lagoon.* Below: *Children ply the Okavango River near Shakawe in their dugout canoe.*

The Stage

Landscapes and waterscapes

The Okavango River springs from a source in the Angolan highlands, and after crossing Namibia's Caprivi Strip it enters Botswana at Mohembo. Thereafter the river's journey takes three distinct forms. The first is known as the Panhandle – the long strip of river and floodplain whose course is set in a southeasterly direction towards the 'pan' of the Delta proper, and within whose broad confines the river meanders in generous loops. After the waters spill over the Gomare Fault, where the land subsided millions of years ago, the river takes on the appearance of a delta, splitting into an intricate web of channels dotted with tree-fringed islands. However, the Okavango is not, strictly speaking, a delta at all, but rather an alluvial fan: instead of discharging into a body of water, as an authentic delta does, the Okavango's channels filter into the thirsty sands of the Kalahari. The fan itself comprises two distinct parts – the permanently and seasonally flooded areas. The permanent or perennial Delta retains water all year round and is clad in a verdant coat of reeds, grasses, shrubs and trees, while the seasonal Delta, apart from its main channels, is a grassland area for much of the year, until the annual floodwaters from torrential summer rains in the Angolan highlands course through the area each winter and transform it briefly into a lush wetland wilderness.

Although the Delta is set within the semi-arid Kalahari, the local climate differs somewhat from that of the surrounding area, in much the same way as mini-climates occur over rainforests. There are marked seasonal differences: temperatures range from 18 °C to 32 °C in summer, and from 5 °C to 25 °C in winter. Annual rainfall at the base of the Delta is around 500 millimetres, and increases towards the source. This in itself is subject to considerable annual fluctuations, which depend largely on southern Africa's fickle weather patterns.

THE PANHANDLE

Shortly after crossing its first international border, into the Caprivi region of Namibia, the Okavango River tumbles over the kilometre-wide rocky quartzite ledge known as the Popa Falls. These are better described as a series of rapids than an actual waterfall, though, the drop that forms the rapids being a mere 4 metres. This is the last time that the waters of the Okavango touch rock: beyond lie the sands of the Kalahari and the river's eventual death in the desert. Immediately to the south, however, herds of elephant bathe and quench their thirst as the river passes through Namibia's Mahango National Park. Although this is certainly not the last opportunity for wildlife to enjoy its life-giving bounty, their territory is abruptly cut short by the fence at Mohembo, which marks the border with Botswana.

When the Okavango enters the Panhandle its flow is contained between two parallel faults, set at right angles to the more southerly faults that created the Delta proper. The Panhandle's faults confine the river's meanderings to a floodplain between two high, forested banks of Kalahari sand, set about 15 kilometres apart. For most of its way, the water flows through the Panhandle in a single broad channel, 90 metres wide and almost 100 kilometres long, dividing only briefly at Nxamaseri before the two strands reunite farther south at Sepupa. It winds across the floodplain in a series of exaggerated S-bends, occasionally cutting through the narrow neck formed by a tight bend in the river and isolating the wide loop to form an ox-bow lake.

Each year about 11 billion cubic metres of water courses through the Panhandle, the sluggish flow reaching its peak towards the end of summer (February–March), months after the first rains have fallen on the Angolan highlands far to the northwest. The flood-waters are contained by the Panhandle's relatively narrow shoulders, and this raises the water level by as much as 2 metres. The Delta region's rainfall is much less than that of its distant catchment area, but the rains that fall between November and April never-theless add a further 5 billion cubic metres of water to the wetland system. Although the figures sound generous, they are deceptive: an astonishing amount of the moisture is lost to the atmosphere or simply disappears into the burning desert sands. In a dry year all the water is lost this way, and even in good years a bare 2 percent of the inflow eventually leaves the Delta system at its base, flowing into the Thamalakane River.

The character of the Delta probably owes more to its flora than to any other single element; without the influence of its vegetation the region would probably amount to little more than a vast salt lake. The area's most ubiquitous plant is papyrus (*Cyperus papyrus*), a tall, fast-growing sedge which dominates the permanent Delta and colonises the banks of the wide Panhandle channel. Here, as in other faster-flowing channels, conditions are ideal for the growth of papyrus, but little else survives as the continuous movement of bedload along the channel floor prevents most other species from taking root.

Along with the water, the river brings an additional load in the form of sediment, of which there are three distinct types: sand eroded from the catchment area and carried along the riverbed as bedload; plant material and fine particles of clay held in suspension in the water; and various chemical compounds. Together, these contribute a staggering 650 000 tonnes or more of load that is carried into the Delta each year, and the water in the Panhandle is murky as a result.

Opposite top: *Namibia's Popa Falls in the fading light of dusk. The Falls are formed by a rocky quartzite ledge and mark the start of the Panhandle.* Opposite bottom and overleaf: *Fishermen return home to Shakawe in their* mekoro, *the region's traditional dugout canoes.* Right: *The Okavango's many forms. The broad sweep of the Panhandle's meanders, flanked by lush swampland and the occasional lagoon, is quite a different environment from the Delta proper, where the water spreads out in a maze of ill-defined channels* (second from top), *punctuated by islands* (bottom), *and where a wide variety of vegetation thrives.*

The channel margins consist of peat (an accumulation of decomposed vegetation), which is stabilised by papyrus and reeds. The peat is permeable, and even when the river level is low, water seeps through it into the surrounding floodplain, for beyond the papyrus-fringed banks in the Panhandle and permanent Delta lie extensive permanently flooded areas. These backwaters embrace a variety of habitats populated largely by floating aquatic plants and water-tolerant grasses and sedges. When the water from the swamps rejoins the main channel farther downstream the material it brings from the floodplains is reintroduced into the channels as suspended load. Of the immense load that the river carries along its journey, about 90 percent is deposited in the upper half of the Panhandle. Sand bars form on the inner bends of channels, while the outer bends get eroded, and this leads to further exaggeration of the meander belt – the path followed by the river as it makes its convoluted way downstream. When the water level in the river drops during the dry season the sand bars are exposed and form important breeding sites for crocodiles and African skimmers. Just how much the river's course fluctuates is clearly indicated in the relic meander belts of the floodplains, though at present they are fairly stable.

As well as being subject to the annual floodwaters from the Angolan highlands for many millennia, the Panhandle area has for much of its modern history accommodated floods of a different nature – waves of human refugees from conflict-ridden

Top: *Day's end on the Okavango River in the Panhandle.* Above: *A motorboat crosses Qhaaxhwa lagoon carrying a load of reeds or* lethaka. *In Delta villages* lethaka *stems are commonly woven together to form large mats or walls.* Opposite: *A tangle of sand bars, formed when the mass of bedload carried by the river is dropped at the mouth of a lagoon.*

areas beyond Botswana's borders who subsequently established villages here. Both Hambukushu and Mbanderu (Herero) people settled along the western edge of the Panhandle during the nineteenth century, and in the late 1960s a further group of Hambukushu immigrants came from war-torn Angola. The groupings in which they gathered while waiting for the Botswanan government to grant them asylum formed the core of the southern Panhandle's thirteen Etsha villages.

Human settlement in the Panhandle introduced new kinds of activity, and today agriculture, fishing and cattle are central to the area's economy. While some traditional fishing and farming practices continue, intervention by international aid agencies has led to significant changes, especially in fishing methods. The extent to which donated motorised fishing craft, gill nets and large commercial freezers – which have led to a dramatic increase in the fishing take in the Panhandle – affect the region's fish stock remains to be seen. The weaving of intricately decorated baskets has also become an important local business. The Hambukushu immigrants of the 1960s made a significant contribution to the revival of the craft and its commercialisation, and these days local basketwork is marketed successfully around the world. The most important industry to have developed here in the last few decades, however, is tourism. The lodges that are dotted along the Panhandle, most of them accessible from the tarred road that runs along the western edge of the Delta, cater primarily for angling and

Above: *Wild date palms fringe the edge of one of the Delta's many islands. The growth of such vegetation slowly enlarges the islands.* Left: *Day waterlilies colonise most of the Okavango's stiller waters, providing platforms for foraging waterbirds.* Below: *A herd of red lechwe bounds across a shallow floodplain.*

birding enthusiasts, and offer boat rides through the Panhandle as well as trips to the nearby Tsodilo Hills.

The human presence, though, has had its impact on the environment, with a noticeable decline in wildlife numbers along the periphery of the Okavango. Although aquatic animals such as crocodile and hippo can still be found in the greater Okavango river system, of the antelope in the area it is only the more elusive, such as the swamp-dwelling sitatunga, that still survive in the Panhandle.

THE PERENNIAL DELTA

Beyond the village of Seronga the nature of the Okavango

Above: Mokoro *stations are commonly seen along the inhabited waterways near the Etsha 6 village. When not in use, the craft are removed from the water, both to slow rotting and to prevent them from floating away.*

wetter climatic period when, owing to the greater volume of water in the system, channel flow in the Delta matched that of the present Panhandle. Today though, channels no longer have the flow strength or volume to form meanders, largely because so much water is lost to the flanking swamps. Although most of the bedload carried into the Okavango system is deposited in the Panhandle, that which is carried downstream is deposited on the channel beds, raising their level, and water seeps out through the permeable channel margins continuously. Dead plant matter that is carried in suspension in the water becomes trapped both on the

River changes dramatically as it passes over the Gomare Fault. This fault forms the northwestern edge of the depression which contains the permanent swamp, a 6 000-square-kilometre wetland where the Okavango assumes the character for which it is famed – a confusion of channels, floodplains, lagoons and islands. Entering the Delta, the waters of the Okavango flow as a river for the last time, the slightly convex form of the land causing the river to split into a series of channels that spread out over a wide area. The gradient, though, is very slight, the water dropping only 65 metres during the entire course of its 250-kilometre journey to Maun. Relic meander belts which scar the surface of the permanent swamp bear witness to a much

channel margins and within the reedbeds between channels. Layers of peat build up in the swampy areas around active channel systems, frequently reaching a thickness of 5 metres. As the load carried in the channels is deposited or captured by reedbeds the clarity of the water improves – downstream the channels become narrower and deeper and the water is quite clear. Past Seronga the river splits into three main distributary systems: the Thaoge to the south, the Jao-Boro system in the centre, and the Nqoga-Maunachira-Mboroga-Santantadibe system to the east. These channel systems serve as the Delta's arteries, providing an essential supply of water that sustains the permanently swampy areas.

Top: *Dwarfed by real fan palms, a herd of elephant leaves a pan after drinking and bathing.* Above: *Near Mohembo, a group of children on their way to fish playfully wear their woven fishing baskets as hats.*

The first of the three distributaries, the Thaoge, used to flow strongly to the south, diverting much of the Delta's water to the massive Lake Ngami. In fact, when Livingstone encountered the lake on his 1849 expedition it was over 100 kilometres in circumference. Three years later the Swedish naturalist Charles Andersson journeyed up the Thaoge for a month, and so became the first European to enter the Okavango Delta proper. Exactly how far up the Thaoge he went before taking another channel farther into the wetlands is a matter of speculation, but he described it as 'deep and wide'. Within a few decades, however, flow to the distal end of the Thaoge had ceased. As recently as the 1970s Lake Ngami filled in times of exceptional rains, but today it is unrecognisable. When viewed from a nearby hill there is nothing to see but bushveld: what was once a sizeable lake has now been reclaimed by the Kalahari, and the only hint of the vast quantities of water it once held are the rain puddles that form alongside the slippery clay road that traverses the dry lakebed.

With the dying of the Thaoge channel various schemes were devised in an attempt to re-establish the water supply to Lake Ngami. At the time it was thought that papyrus blockages upstream had halted the flow, but it is now accepted that channels have a limited life span: the constant change of water distribution within the Delta – with the drying up of some channels and the consequent switching of flow to others – is an integral part of the system's self-renewal, and the growth of dense papyrus stands is a product, rather than the cause, of the failing process. Fanciful attempts at reviving the moribund channel were thus doomed from the start. Among various options considered for removing the blockages were a simple scheme to cut them out by hand, the construction of weirs to cut off water flow to the papyrus stands, after which the dead vegetation was to be burnt, and finally an extravagant design for a giant papyrus-cutting machine. Funds were also scarce, and in the end all these schemes proved futile. Today the Thaoge still captures about 16 percent of the river's flow, but the water supply falters long before it reaches Lake Ngami.

Described in the 1930s as a 'wasteful' channel, the Boro River began to flow strongly in 1952, an event which may well have been caused by a major earthquake that occurred nearby in that year. Currently the Jao-Boro system takes about a quarter of the Okavango's flow and is the main arterial channel to the west of Chief's Island in the central Delta area.

The remainder of the flow is concentrated in the Nqoga-Maunachira-Mboroga-Santantadibe system. At present this is the Delta system's major distributary, though despite this impressive status the channel is also undergoing change. Originally the

Right: *One of the many subsistence farms scattered along the waterways of the western Delta.* Below: *Occasionally, while travelling along the narrow, papyrus-roofed Okavango channels, one encounters larger expanses of water such as Guma Lagoon.*

Nqoga (the eastern arm of the Okavango River) fed directly into the Mboroga Channel, which runs southeastwards past Chief's Island, but it is now in the process of failure and currently flows into the Maunachira system, which carries water to Khwai on the eastern edge of the Moremi Game Reserve. Although there is a narrow connecting channel between the Mboroga-Santantadibe and Maunachira systems, most water transferred from one to the other is filtered through the surrounding swamps.

Failure seems to be an inevitable part of the life cycle of a channel, estimated to last about 200 years from formation to failure. The process is understood to occur along the following lines. Although water flows constantly through the permeable channel margins, the vegetation along the edges prevents bedload from leaving the channel. The bedload is deposited on the channel bed, and gradually the entire system is raised higher and higher above the surrounding swamp, at a rate of about 5 centimetres a year. The difference in height between the channel surface and the surrounding areas causes water loss to increase, and flow within the channel slows down. Hippo grass (*Vossia cuspidata*) prospers in these conditions and its growth encroaches on the channel, trapping papyrus debris generated upstream. Rafts of debris accumulate as individual pieces become entangled, and are commonly seen floating along the Delta's waterways. With more and more water being lost to the surrounding swamps, there is a dramatic rise in the growth and density of papyrus on the channel margins. Along with the blockages caused by floating vegetation, this dense papyrus growth on the channel fringes provides a further obstacle to the water in the channel system, which then seeks out paths of lesser resistance upstream. Often it will flow into the well-worn trails made by hippo and elephant as they move through the swamps. With the increased volume of water entering these trails they become enlarged and eventually form new channel systems.

Meanwhile, vegetation blockages and channel failure gradually progress upstream, and eventually flow to the distal ends of the channels ceases altogether. With its essential water supply cut off the swamp begins to desiccate, and the dried-out peat becomes susceptible to fire. The smouldering fires that burn within the peat deposits are catalysts in the transformation of these areas from swamps to nutrient-rich grasslands, following the paths of the failing channel upstream and typically reducing the 4–5-metre-thick layer of peat to 30 centimetres of fertile ash. The grasses that subsequently grow here attract other natural agents that continue the conversion process: herds of large herbivores enter the area and enrich it with their droppings, while termites distribute the peat ash through the subsurface. After the fires, the former channel beds, which were raised above the level of the surrounding areas by the constant deposit of bedload, appear as elevated sandbanks. The process of change continues unabated; eventually these grassland areas become flooded again and the raised former channels provide the foundations for the formation of islands.

In addition to the channels, larger expanses of open water are found throughout the Okavango, mostly in the permanently flooded areas. In wetter times meander belts, much like that of the Panhandle, are formed, and when the area dries out again, they appear as ridges of sand. For part of its journey the Maunachira Channel follows the Xugana meander ridge, thought to be between 2 000 and 3 000 years old. Where the Maunachira flows through this area it floods relic ox-bows, forming large lakes (locally known as *madiba*) such as Xugana and Gcodikwe. In other cases, such as Xakanaxa Lediba, lakes are formed when water dams up against raised parts of the meander belt. Over time, those lakes that are directly connected to channel systems fill with sediment, which builds up particularly at the entrance to the lake. Eventually the lakes either become conventional channels or are bypassed completely. Bypassed lakes have to rely on the influx of water from surrounding swamps for their continued existence, but are known to persist for long periods.

The sediment-filled lake entrances provide an ideal environment for the growth of aquatic plants, the most commonly encountered of which are the water chestnut (*Trapa natans*), easily identifiable with its triangular 'toothed' leaves, and the day waterlily (*Nymphaea nouchali caerulea*). To keep themselves afloat both plants have developed tiny air bladders – within the leaves of the water chestnut and in the stalks of the day waterlily. This waterlily is a common sight in most still, open water areas in the Delta, where its stately blue, white and pink flowers provide

Above: *Disturbed while feeding on a mat of papyrus, a young sitatunga ram stares warily at us as we pass on our* mokoro. Opposite: *Viewed from the air, distinctive bands of vegetation can be seen on one of the Okavango's myriad islands.*

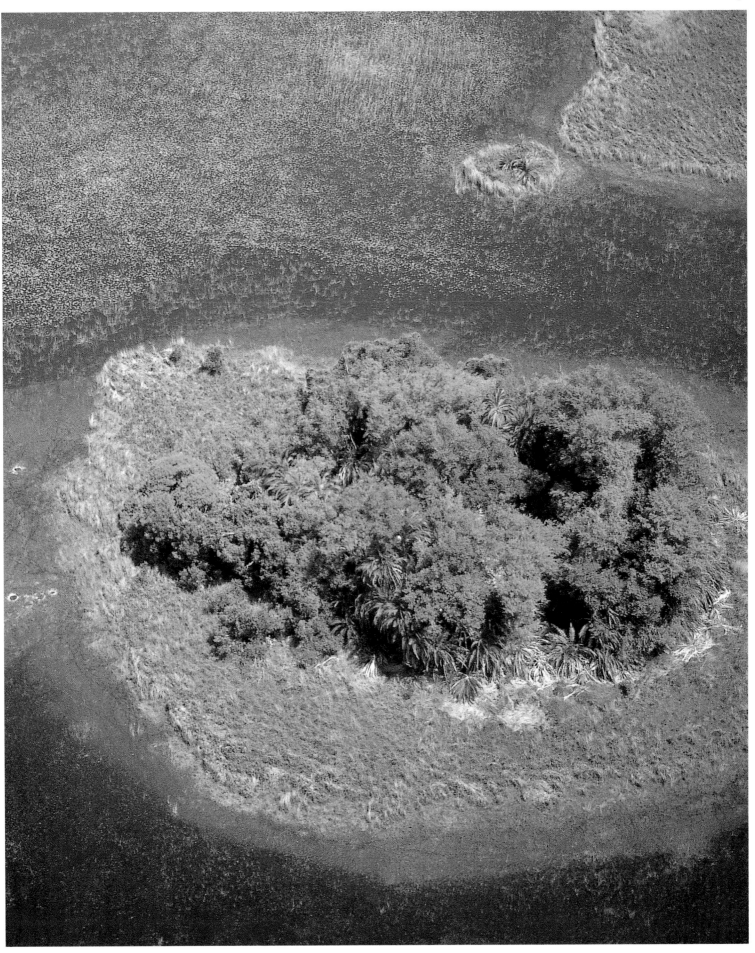

Previous pages: *The fine strands of a spider's web, strung between stalks of cottonwool grass, are etched in the golden sunlight.* Above: *A band of lush riverine forest surrounds the Mmaleswana Pan, a permanent body of water which captures overflow from Xakanaxa Lagoon.*

an accent of colour on the water surface. Unopened lily buds are held on coiled stems beneath the water until they are ready to flower. The flowers surface and remain open during the day until they are pollinated, after which they are drawn underwater again. Here the fruit ripens, and when it eventually disintegrates the seeds are dispersed. The day waterlily's less visible nocturnal relative, the night waterlily (*Nymphaea lotus*), bears yellow flowers which open in the late afternoon. Its leaves act as stepping-stones for a variety of waterbirds to use when foraging along the waterways, and can be told from those of the day waterlily by their serrated margins. The plant is also a source of nourishment for the tiny pygmy goose, whose diet consists almost exclusively of lily fruits.

The arrival of the seasonal flood in the Delta does not bring the dramatic rise in water level that is usual in the Panhandle. At the Jao-Boro intersection, for instance, the water rises a mere 15 centimetres. As the floods are not confined they spread out slowly across the fan, taking a full four months to get to the far reaches of the Delta: if its flow were confined to channels, the flood's 250-kilometre journey would last a mere ten days.

Some years the head of the flood reaches Maun, and the water that remains after its passage through the Delta dams up against the Thamalakane Fault, creating the Thamalakane River. In years of heavy flooding the waters can reach the Boteti River, which runs through a break in the fault and flows out to the

Makgadikgadi Pans some distance to the southeast, or – very occasionally – make their way southwards to Lake Ngami. Even in a good year the volume of water leaving the system (as both outflow and seepage into groundwater) is a tiny fraction of the immense quantity that entered it: almost all of the water is lost through transpiration and evaporation.

With such a huge loss, one would expect the water leaving the Delta system to be extremely saline, but in fact the salinity level barely doubles during the course of its journey, and saline surface water within the swamps is very rare. This remarkable state of affairs is due largely to the proliferation of islands throughout the Delta, which effectively act as the swamps' detoxification centres.

An estimated 50 000 islands are scattered throughout the Okavango Delta, ranging in area from a single square metre to 1 000 square kilometres. They are formed in a variety of ways, most developing from small nuclei. Some begin as elevated features like termite mounds, or as abandoned channel beds that stand proud after fires have reduced the surrounding peat to a thin layer of ash. Their original shape is usually etched in their eventual form, so islands that nucleate on termite mounds are invariably round, while those formed on former channel beds tend to be narrow and sinuous. Other islands – the massive Chief's Island being a notable example – are the result of tectonic activity.

The reason salinity levels are low is that most water loss occurs by transpiration (that is, by the 'breathing' of the many plants here), rather than by direct evaporation. When trees transpire, salts present in the water are left behind in the ground-water. Water from the surrounding swamp seeps into the ground beneath the islands to replace the water removed by the trees, and with continual transpiration the salinity of the groundwater under the islands increases to such an extent that the salts

Above: *Transformation of the seasonal Delta: after the summer rains, autumn, and the arrival of the annual flood in winter.* Below left: *In winter, the sticky remains of a drying pan seem to hold a hippo herd captive.* Below right: *Summer rains inundate depressions throughout dryland Okavango.*

eventually precipitate between the subsurface sand grains. As a result, the sand grains are forced apart and the land surface rises. Saturation occurs in the middle of smaller islands and just in from the edges of larger islands. As the salt-laden areas grow in size, the vegetation becomes concentrated on the island fringes and over time this contributes to the expansion of the islands.

Levels of toxicity vary across each island: whereas high concentrations of salts make the centre the most toxic part, the constantly expanding fringes are usually healthier. Consequently islands have distinct bands of vegetation: the margins are characterised by wild date palms, which surround a densely vegetated zone dominated by broad-leafed evergreens such as

sycamore figs (*Ficus sycomorus*) and jackalberries (*Diospyros mespiliformis*). The latter, one of the Okavango's largest trees, is commonly used in the manufacture of the area's traditional dugout canoes. Still farther in towards the island's centre one finds knobthorns (*Acacia nigrescens*) and large feverberries (*Croton megalobotrys*), while the vegetation closest to the salt-laden centres consists of salt-tolerant species like real fan palms (*Hyphaene petersiana*), whose leaves are used for making basket-ware. These elegant palms are perfectly adapted to their salty environment, and the rustling of their fans in the wind is a characteristic and evocative island sound. Some island centres are dominated by spike grass (*Sporobolus spicatus*), which often

has small salt crystals on its leaves. On other islands even the most salt-tolerant species are unable to survive, and the interior consists of a totally barren central pan.

When the groundwater reaches these levels of toxicity, trees start to die and capillary action brings the saline water to the surface where it evaporates, leaving behind a white, powdery crust of sodium bicarbonate which can be seen on most island interiors. Inevitably, though, channel failure prevents water from flowing to the areas of swamp surrounding these islands, the water table

mekoro trips and game-viewing walks on the region's many islands. Exploring the region's wildlife in this fashion – either on foot or from the waters – provides a refreshingly intimate experience of the Okavango.

Although human settlement is generally less dense in the permanent Delta than elsewhere, there is, in addition to the lodges, a large village at Jedibe and several small settlements scattered along the western fringes of the Delta. Here, a number of Hambukushu people live on islands along the channels,

Above: *The different faces of the Moremi Game Reserve floodplains: before and after the life-giving summer rains.* Opposite: *A flock of white-faced ducks circles an Okavango lagoon in search of a suitable place to alight.*

falls and the dead plants can no longer draw salts to the islands. The salts are eventually flushed from the island surface by rain, then funnelled into the subsurface, and they finally seep away into the groundwater. Calcite and silica deposits remain though, and the island form is retained when the area is reflooded.

In this way the islands detoxify the wetlands. Although saline water is also generated by the masses of aquatic plants that inhabit the system, it is thought that this is partly taken in by salt-absorbing bacteria that live in the layers of peat.

Compared with the Panhandle, the permanent Delta supports relatively high densities of wildlife, especially in Moremi Game Reserve and the surrounding areas. The animals here generally keep to the floodplain's myriad islands, some of which are home to quite high concentrations of game. Most species typical of the wider region are represented, notably hippo, crocodile, lechwe and sitatunga, and most of the larger mammals, including predators such as lion and leopard, move regularly between islands. Game-viewing in the permanent Delta, however, is seldom easy, mainly because the ever-present water makes it difficult to move around. A profusion of tourist lodges dot the permanent Delta, bearing evocative (and, to many Westerners, often unpronounceable) names like Nxabega, Xugana and Shindi. Most are situated on islands or on the edge of the permanently flooded zone. Visitor attractions at these lodges typically include

deriving their livelihood from subsistence crop-farming. Spread out as they are along the meandering channels, these small villages rely on passing craft for news – with the lodge motorboats offering the most efficient way of disseminating information, tourists are often stopped for the latest news and messages.

THE SEASONAL DELTA

During summer the woodlands around the Delta are punctuated by numerous rain-filled pools, at which a multitude of animals gather to drink and bathe. In winter these pools slowly disappear, leaving behind cracked clay husks. The animals then turn to the Delta's edge for water, and the surrounding grasslands are cropped low by the constant attention of the grazing herds. Lechwe and flocks of waders and other waterbirds follow the moving edge of the flood, and as the flood reaches the outlying floodplains the seasonal Delta springs to life. The inundation rejuvenates the dry, overgrazed grasslands, and zebra wade into the water to graze the fresh shoots emerging from its surface. Depending on the duration of the flooding, different grasses and sedges make their appearance; slipping over the surface of the shallow waters by *mokoro*, one seems to pass through a veritable mosaic of water-tolerant plant communities. When spring comes, the flood recedes and great herds of herbivores assemble to graze

Above: *Where the Okavango and the Kalahari meet, vegetation more adapted to arid conditions, like this camelthorn, is common.*
Right: *One of the countless species of mushroom that erupt after the summer rains.*

on the new flushes of dryland grasses that begin to cover the drying surface of the floodplains. Wherever these herds gather to feed, spotted hyaena, lion and other predators soon arrive in force to share in the bounty.

Although it is made from the same building blocks as the permanent swamp, the 12 000-square-kilometre area of seasonal swamp appears quite different. It is effectively the transition zone between the Kalahari and the Delta, and so contains the greatest variety of plant and animal species. The islands are bigger here than elsewhere, and a large part of the area is occupied by expansive floodplains. The progression from the permanent to the seasonal Delta is also marked by a change in vegetation: the squat wild date palm (*Phoenix reclinata*) makes way for the tall, elegant real fan palm, and papyrus is no longer dominant. Active channels are now flanked by miscanthus grass (*Miscanthus junceus*), whose leaves have sharp tips and, unless recently burnt, are inedible. The change in vegetation is environmentally important as prolific papyrus growth could cause significant blockages in the seasonal swamp's slow-flowing channels. Miscanthus grass, however, cannot grow over open areas of water: instead, it helps to stabilise channel margins. In addition, there is almost no transport of sediment in these slower waters, and as a result they remain translucent and the beds become vegetated. Water lettuce (*Ottelia ulvifolia*) thrives in this environment, and its long, broad leaves are commonly seen wafting in the clear channels, providing a refuge for small fish.

Most of the seasonally flooded area consists of floodplains, whose appearance changes constantly, depending on the season and the strength of the annual floods. As the floodwaters reach these areas they flow down dry channels and then spread out in a thin layer over the surrounding grasslands. The short-cropped dry grasses are soon submerged and aquatic plants, similar to those found in the permanent Delta, start growing. These newly flooded areas provide fresh feeding and spawning grounds for countless fish, more than eighty species of which are found in the waters of the Okavango, with predatory varieties dominating. One such predator, the African pike, prefers deeper waters but readily enters the flooded *molapos* (as the floodplains are known locally), where it is the main predator. Its close relative the tiger fish is happiest in the rivers and larger lagoons, and catfish are found throughout the region, as are three species of tilapia. A huge variety of storks, herons, waders and shorebirds stalk the fish in the shallows. Later in the season, when the water recedes and the fishes' shrinking habitat becomes increasingly restricted, the birds enjoy even easier feeding.

With the onset of the hot weather the thin sheet of water soon draws back, and aquatic vegetation is replaced by a wealth of new grasses. The floodplains remain relatively open because they are too wet for the larger, woody plant species but do not have enough moisture to encourage the growth of reedbeds. Although some small shrubs may put in an appearance, these are destroyed

Above: *A herd of buffalo grazes on the fringe of the mopane woodland.*
Right: *Ants forage along the stem and in the flower of a wild dagga herb.*

Above: *In the Thamalakane River bed near Maun, children help the last dusty trickle of water from the Delta to flow further.*

Above and below: *Signs of emerging commercialism: Khwai village entrepreneurs respond to the growing tourist trade.*

in the fires that sweep through about three-quarters of the Delta's floodplains each year when the grasses dry out. The dominant grasses are tufted species, while couch grass (*Cynodon dactylon*), a low-growing, creeping perennial, grows on areas of raised ground and is important to the grazing animals. Although floodplain grasses flourish here, the abundance of water encourages rapid growth, and this makes them coarse and relatively poor in nutrients, especially protein. Nevertheless they attract large herds of game since, at this time of year, there is little alternative grazing left and depressions in the floodplains still hold some water. Fish that entered the flooded grasslands are frequently trapped in the shrinking pools and are the object of spectacular feeding frenzies among the bird populations – nearly thirty species were counted at one of these feasts.

At the base of the seasonal Delta lies the town of Maun, whose name means 'place of reeds'. This was once a remote frontier out-post, a village of reed and straw huts, and until quite recently motorists would often get stuck in its sandy streets. All that has now changed, and few reminders of the dusty days remain. Some, such as the mopane pole-and-calcrete Matlapaneng Bridge, over which travellers passed on their way to the northern wilderness, have been declared monuments. Although agriculture and live-stock remain the focus of economic activity in the surrounding villages, many of their inhabitants are involved in the tourism industry and its support services: with the arrival of the tarred road from Francistown, Maun took on a distinctly modern, cosmopolitan image and the town is now the gateway to the Delta.

THE TSODILO HILLS

About 40 kilometres to the west of the Panhandle lies a rocky outcrop known as the Tsodilo Hills. Rising about 400 metres above the dry Kalahari landscape, the hills are renowned for their impressive 'galleries' of delicate sketches portraying animals and hunters. The artists responsible for the more than 3 500 paintings that adorn the overhangs and crevices are unknown: although it is assumed that they were of Bushman origin, the handful of Bushmen that live here today cannot shed any light on their artistic ancestors.

The paintings, which gaze out over the surrounding scrub-covered flatlands from several vantage points, are a poignant reminder of the wealth of animals this area once sustained. Gone are the vast herds of only a few centuries ago – today, the region is virtually devoid of wildlife. Happily, though, deep within the Delta lies a formally protected area where antelope and other animals can still gather at the water's edge, largely undisturbed by the human presence.

MOREMI GAME RESERVE

By the late 1950s environmentalists, authorities and the Batawana people alike had become increasingly concerned about the decline in numbers of game in the Okavango region. Uncontrolled hunting had depleted the region's wildlife resources

– with Tswana hunters viewing the wildlife as an inexhaustible supply of meat, and an additional threat from professional hunters from East Africa seeking fresh hunting grounds – and the need for a formally protected area in the Delta was beginning to be recognised.

In 1963 the wife of the late Batawana chief, Moremi III, declared the Moremi Game Reserve in his honour: it was the first wildlife sanctuary in southern Africa to be set aside, voluntarily, by an African community on their own land. Initially consisting of a triangle of countryside south of the Khwai River,

Above: *Van der Post's Panel, one of the many groups of Bushman paintings that grace the Tsodilo Hills.* Below left and right: *The Okavango's towering woodlands often dwarf their animal inhabitants.*

the reserve was later enlarged by the addition of Chief's Island in the 1970s, and then a further area to the northwest of the island in 1991. Today the reserve covers nearly 5 000 square kilometres, and effectively protects large parts of each landscape component of the Okavango ecosystem.

Historically the area has supported little human habitation because of the widespread presence of tsetse fly in and around the Delta. Although people and their cattle moved into the area when the infestation declined following the 1894 rinderpest epidemic, they were soon driven out again when the fly began to re-establish itself, and within fifty years this tiny but devastating creature had reclaimed most of its original territory. There was, however, a Banoka community living in the area before the reserve was proclaimed – people who had originally come from Seronga at the base of the Panhandle, and who had settled at Xakanaxa and later near Dombo Hippo Pools. When the reserve was declared they relocated to Khwai village.

The reserve is not fenced; rather, it is surrounded by a buffer zone of wildlife management areas and private concessions that offer hunting or photographic safaris, and by the Chobe National Park. Wildlife is free to move between these areas and Moremi, although the distant presence of buffalo fences (designed to prevent contact between wildlife and cattle) everywhere except in the east prevents large-scale migrations from the southern Kalahari regions.

Mopane tongues – strips of land that gain their name from the abundance of mopane trees that grow on them – make up about 80 percent of Moremi's dryland area. The mopane tree (*Colophospermum mopane*) grows on poorly drained soils with a high clay content, its success in this environment due to the ability of its shallow root system to obtain moisture trapped close to the surface. Easily recognised by its butterfly-shaped leaves, it occurs in two ecotypes, or environmentally influenced varieties. One is a tall, V-shaped tree, with a rounded crown, that normally forms single-species woodland; the other is a shorter, multi-stemmed variety that grows as low scrub. The latter is usually found in depressions and typically indicates shallow soil with a calcrete foundation (though stunted growth can also occur because of fire or a lack of nutrients); its density generally makes it poor wildlife habitat. Mopane woodland, on the other hand, is home to large numbers of animals, especially in the wet season. At this time, rainwater pans appear throughout the woodland, and its grasses (typically those tolerant of seasonally waterlogged soils) are sought after by grazing animals. During the rains the availability of both new mopane leaves and sweet, palatable grasses accounts for the absence of large concentrations of game outside the woodlands.

The rainwater pans hold water long into the dry season and are often host to herds of wallowing and drinking buffalo and elephant. The latter are very partial to mopane trees and their presence often hinders the progress of vehicles in areas where these trees are common: elephant tend to follow vehicle tracks for easy passage through the mopaneveld, and will often push trees into the road or simply loiter on the track. Tourist roads to the more enticing areas of Moremi, which pass through seemingly

Heedless of the approaching thunderstorm, a breeding herd of elephant feeds on the rainy season's flush of new grasses in Moremi Game Reserve.

endless stands of mopane, become even more treacherous in the wet season, when the clay soil traps water in depressions. During periods of heavy rain, the depressions are invisible and the entire track becomes an unbroken sheet of water. Driving in these conditions is not for the faint-hearted. Another hazard one encounters in the mopaneveld is apparently suicidal tree squirrels that frequently dash across one's path – and roadside squirrel carcasses are a common sight.

Holes form naturally in the trunks of mopane trees and provide homes not only for the very visible tree squirrel, but also for a host of other rodents and nesting birds. At night, the profusion of nocturnal rodents draws large numbers of owls to the woodlands. During the day Burchell's starling (*Lamprotornis australis*) and Arnot's chat (*Thamnolaea arnoti*) – a bird found almost exclusively in mopane woodlands – are the most commonly encountered avian species.

In the heat of the day it is often difficult to find shade in the mopane woodland, as the mopane leaves fold in half and hang vertically to reduce water loss. These leaves provide sustenance for various insects, probably the best known of which is the mopane worm – the larva of a type of emperor moth (*Gonimbrasia belina*), it is prized as a delicacy in parts of southern Africa. The caterpillars hatch after three weeks and immediately devour their eggshell – which is thought to contain an enzyme that kickstarts the caterpillar's digestive system – and for the rest of their lives they feed exclusively on mopane leaves. The tiny larvae of a psyllid insect also depend on the leaves, not only eating them (which is thought to make the leaves curl) but also making their home beneath waxy scales which they create on the surface of the leaves. These scales are much sought after by primates, and vervet monkeys and baboons can often be seen nibbling them off the leaves.

Towards the permanent waterways and the northern edge of the Moremi Game Reserve the mopane woodland gives way to a ring of mixed marginal woodland, floodplain and riverine forest, the most spectacular parts of which are found at Khwai and Xakanaxa. The Maunachira-Khwai river system, which runs alongside the northern boundary, forms the eastern arm of the Okavango channel network. Situated near the northeastern boundary of the reserve, the Khwai area is graced by wide floodplains and walls of tall forest that fringe the mopane woodland beyond. At its centre is North Gate – the northern entry point into the reserve from the neighbouring Chobe National Park. The village of Khwai lies across the timber bridge at North Gate; originally established by the Banoka people who were displaced when the reserve was proclaimed, it is now a sizeable settlement. The presence of the river and its extensive floodplain makes the Khwai area an exceptional spot for game-viewing, especially in the winter months when the pools within the mopane woodlands have dried up. At this time of year, even those animals that prefer to stay within the canopy of the surrounding woodlands have to cross open country to drink at the river. The floodplains that flank the river here are dotted with innumerable termite mounds, each invariably

surmounted by a francolin, hornbill or roller. Significantly, the region was one of the first areas in Botswana to host photographic safaris, but this kind of tourism became really popular only after the tsetse fly had been eradicated from the area in the early 1980s.

Upstream from Khwai lies the Xakanaxa area, where the landscapes are at their most varied. Seldom do forests, pans, islands and floodplains all combine in one small area, yet in dryland Xakanaxa one can easily pass through each of these habitats on a short game drive. Three private lodges and a public campsite are situated here; all are set on the edge of the Xakanaxa Lediba, a lake that formed when the rivers of the Delta dammed up against a relic meander belt. Boat trips on the nearby lagoon and game drives through the area are popular pastimes here, and it is also, incidentally, arguably one of the best places in the Delta for seeing leopard. The lake is home to dense thickets of water fig (*Ficus verruculosa*), a small bushy tree that commonly grows along the Delta's waterways. In the lakes, however, the plant has managed to establish itself in shallow areas, forming thickets that provide ideal cover in which large colonies of egrets, herons, storks and ibises can nest. Over time the accumulation of bird droppings has formed firm bases for the trees. The fig thickets are ideal for roosting as well as nesting,

Opposite: *Elephants are particularly partial to mopane, and the shattered branches that are found throughout the mopane woodland bear witness to their passing.* Above and left: *Typical scenes from the mopane woodland: a young lion lazing in the dappled shade, and a cluster of tree squirrels on a termite mound.*

and at sunset large flocks of birds descend on them. With evening comes a cacophony of sounds from the roosting birds, and this, together with the glories of the day's last light, provide an unforgettable experience.

South of the lodges is a band of lofty riverine forest which in places is reminiscent of an English park that has been tended by a careful groundsman. On elevated fringes around the waterways the trees grow close together, their roots supplied with abundant water but free from waterlogging. As there are so many trees competing for light, though, their crowns are small and interlocked. Jackalberries, sausage trees (*Kigelia africana*) and mangosteens (*Garcinia livingstonei*) are prominent residents of this area.

The riverine forest gives way to mopane woodland to the east, and a series of pans and floodplains farther to the south. To the west of the pans is Goaxhlo Island, an eerie place of drowned tree stumps set alongside a large pan. Game-viewing here can be frustrating – animal concentrations are constantly shifting, and the presence of numerous islands amidst a maze of waterways also leaves many parts of the region inaccessible. However, the mix of habitats makes Xakanaxa an unbeatable birding area, and a place which must surely be among the most beautiful on earth.

To the southwest of Xakanaxa is an area called Third Bridge, whose name is a reference to the mopane pole crossing found here. Its campsite, set within the tall riverine forest, offers possibly the best wilderness experience in Moremi. Lions regularly use the bridge to cross the narrow stream that flows through the camp, so it is often unnecessary to leave the grounds for game-watching experiences! The area lies outside the mopane tongue and consists for the most part of relatively open grasslands and acacia woodland. Game-viewing here can be spectacular at times, especially along the road south of Third Bridge towards the reserve's southern entry point at Maqwee. A string of large pools surrounded by floodplains attracts impressive herds of herbivores, and the resident lions often make kills around the waterholes.

Chief's Island, flanked by the Boro and Santantadibe rivers, is separated from dryland Moremi by permanent floodplains. Roughly 1 000 square kilometres in extent, this is the largest expanse of solid land within the Okavango Delta, and is thought to have been formed by tectonic uplift. The island was originally the principal hunting ground of Chief Moremi, but is now part of the game reserve that bears his name. Buffalo are particularly fond of its central parts, where the abundant acacia thornscrub and mopane woodlands provide good cover. The grasses that grow here on the island's Kalahari sandveld are sweeter than the coarser floodplain species, and this, together with the rainwater pans of the clay areas, attracts large concentrations of game. A number of private lodges have access to Chief's Island, most of them set on its southern shores.

Against a serene backdrop of riverine forest, a kudu bull strolls along the water's edge.

The Cast

Creatures of an African oasis

Lion

The Okavango's annual flood, which gathers momentum between January and March, is a gentle rather than spectacular sequence: the waters that make their slow way down from the Panhandle to inundate the slightly lower-lying plains take several months to reach their southern extremity. But it is a regular event, progenitor of the seasonal rhythms, its ebb and flow continually changing the face of the land. Each year the wetlands are regenerated, taking on new life after the long dry months.

This process of renewal, together with the many habitat types, enables the Delta and its surrounds to support a remarkable number and diversity of life forms, among them 164 species of mammal, more than 400 of bird, 157 of reptile, 84 kinds of fish and over 5 000 of insect. But, for all that, the Delta is not considered a prime wildlife region. The apparent lushness of the terrain is deceptive: this is part of the wider Kalahari system and the soils are sandy, poor in nutrients; the plant communities are not as productive as one might expect; the carrying capacity of the grasslands is much lower than that of such wildlife havens as, say, the Serengeti-Mara area of East Africa. Moreover, hunting and various forms of commercial exploitation – including cattle expansion and misguided attempts to eradicate the tsetse fly – have exerted heavy pressure on an already fragile environment. Only in the Moremi Game Reserve, a largely dryland area, do the game populations reach densities comparable to those of Africa's major sanctuaries.

It is impossible, in a book of this kind, to do justice to all the Delta's living forms. Those illustrated in the following pages represent the more characteristic of the region's residents – the cast of 'players' most frequently encountered in this wetland wilderness arena.

MAMMALS

The most visibly evident of the Okavango Delta's extensive wildlife complement – and arguably the region's star attraction – are the mammals. Among them are four of the so-called Big Five (originally a hunting term used to describe Africa's most dangerous species, and now prime quarry of the visiting game-viewer), namely lion, leopard, elephant, buffalo and rhino. Tragically, the rhino has been relentlessly persecuted, poached to the brink of extinction for its horn, and nowhere in Botswana has it survived in the wild. But in addition to these impressive and eye-catching species, the varied habitats of the Okavango are also populated by a wide range of other mammals, including such diverse creatures as the stately giraffe and highly strung tree squirrels (the delight of many a visitor to the region's campsites and lodges), delicate, agile antelope and portly hippos that wallow in the mud of the Delta's myriad waterways.

HIPPOPOTAMUS

The largest amphibious inhabitant of the Okavango region, the hippopotamus (*Hippopotamus amphibius*) is a familiar sight in the Delta. Second in mass only to the elephant, an average adult weighs approximately 1 500 kilograms. Its ears, eyes and nostrils appear as raised protuberances so that its primary senses are still effective when its body is submerged. It will readily show its displeasure at passing boats in a characteristic yawning gesture that shows the formidable teeth set in the lower jaw. Hippo graze predominantly at night, treading well-worn paths to reach regular feeding grounds. Although almost comical in appearance and seemingly slow and clumsy, these creatures can be bad-tempered and very dangerous, and the local people know to treat them with a great deal of respect.

Historically, this animal has been extensively hunted, mainly for its meat and teeth (which are similar to elephant ivory), and hippo populations were once severely depleted throughout southern Africa. The Bayei used to hunt hippo from their *mekoro*, impaling an animal with barbed harpoons and allowing themselves to be dragged over the water by the wounded victim in the hope of spearing it to death before it killed them. Another method employed to capture hippo was to booby-trap the animals' well-used trails by

suspending a heavily weighted spear above the track. Losses caused by hunting were compounded when the hippopotamus was also drawn into the crocodile-hunting industry, in which hippo carcasses were reputedly used as bait.

Despite these depredations, however, hippo are still readily seen in the Delta. Single hippo often take up residence in the rain pans that form in the bush during the wet season. As these and other pools gradually dry out at the edges of the Delta, groups sometimes gather in deeper, more permanent pools, dispersing at night to feed. Although large pods of hippo are rare, these animals are sometimes seen *en masse* in deeper water, trying to keep their bodies submerged in the coolth. A hippo can remain underwater for several minutes at a stretch, and may surprise the unsuspecting visitor with a blast of spray as it lets out its breath and surfaces again. Although its hide and fatty tissue are about 5 centimetres thick, the hippo is basically hairless and its epidermis is very thin and lacks sweat glands. It must therefore keep cool by staying submerged or wallowing in mud. A glandular secretion that makes the animal appear to be sweating blood works much like sunblock in preventing sunburn.

ELEPHANT

The African elephant (*Loxodonta africana*) is certainly the most distinctive of the Okavango's – and indeed of Africa's – animals. Weighing in at between 4 000 and 7 000 kilograms, it is by far the largest land mammal, as well as being among the most sociable of animals. The basic unit is a breeding herd presided over by a cow, or matriarch, and consisting largely of her female relatives and their offspring. Elephant bulls leave the herd as adolescents and live as bachelors, either alone or in association with other bulls, though dominant and sexually active bulls normally remain in contact with the breeding herd.

Although there are an estimated 71 000 elephant in northern Botswana, many of their number live outside the Okavango system – some sources estimate that as few as 10 percent actually visit the Delta itself. During the dry season, however, relatively large breeding herds congregate around the remaining permanent water and on the outskirts of the seasonal flood, the Khwai River and Santawani regions being favourite haunts. At this time, the animals become important agents of change within the Okavango as they wade out into the channels and lagoons to feed on *Phragmites* reed roots and to drink, flattening reedbeds as they go. As a result of their movements, they create paths that can eventually become new water channels. The elephant's large size and unique trunk enable it to feed on plant material from beneath ground level to higher than even a giraffe can reach – not without reason is it known as 'the world's most versatile herbivore'. This versatility is crucial to survival, as an individual must consume about 150 kilograms of plant material and 160 litres of water each day in order to thrive. Such demands have a massive impact on the Okavango environment: in addition to the potential channels elephant create as they move through the swamps, their tendency to uproot or ring-bark trees as they feed inevitably results in habitat modification. When tree destruction becomes widespread, woodlands are opened up and, with continued pressure, can eventually become grasslands. Whether this is beneficial to the elephant's environment or not is a matter of some debate – one which is linked to the merits or otherwise of culling excess elephant populations in conservation areas.

Botswana's elephant have characteristically small tusks, probably a result of a nutrient deficiency in their diet. Despite this, the elephant was a frequent victim in the days when commercial hunting was at its peak in the Delta region. Ivory was among the commodities most sought after, and innumerable tusks made their way back to Europe to be fashioned into piano keys, billiard balls, jewellery and the like. Today, the elephant population of Botswana is very healthy, perhaps too healthy – it is considered in some quarters to be higher than the region's carrying capacity, and calls have been made in some quarters to begin culling operations. However, popular opinion remains opposed to this option, and as yet no such moves have been made.

WETLAND ANTELOPE

The Delta is home to three semi-aquatic antelope – the sitatunga (*Tragelaphus spekei*), the red lechwe (*Kobus leche*) and the waterbuck (*K. ellipsiprymnus*), the latter two of which belong to the kob family (*Kobus*, a subgroup of the Reduncinae subfamily). Although all of these animals are dependent on water, they are not amphibious.

The Okavango Delta forms the southernmost limit of the sitatunga's range, which extends northwards into the wetlands of East and Central Africa. The only antelope to be confined to the permanently inundated areas of the Delta, the sitatunga is predominantly a grazing animal, surviving largely on the papyrus sedge that grows in abundance in these parts. Its fondness for papyrus, however, makes it vulnerable to the practice of periodic reed-burning, which severely reduces its source of both food and cover. The sitatunga is well adapted to its aquatic environs: the animal's 18-centimetre-long hooves splay out as its weight is transferred onto them, enabling it to move comfortably amongst the reedbeds, through mud and on floating vegetation. It will also eat while partially or fully submerged. To reach its feeding grounds this antelope uses regular paths, although it seldom moves through those made by hippos as crocodiles sometimes lurk in the area. Its shaggy brown coat and curled horns make it easy to identify, but under normal circumstances it is seen only by the fortunate few, even in areas where the animal is abundant. After fires, however, large gatherings of sitatunga will often appear on blackened reedbeds, attracted by fresh shoots, especially those of *Phragmites*. During the day sitatunga usually rest in the reedbeds on platforms

Red lechwe ram

of trampled vegetation, and are easily spotted from the air.

Southern Africa's largest red lechwe population, some 30 000 strong, resides in the Delta area. Favouring the floodplains that border the swamp, this antelope moves extensively as it follows the edge of the seasonal flood. Although not as specialised as the sitatunga, it has similarly splayed hooves that enable it to move faster through shallow water than on dry land. For this reason the animals readily take to water to escape potential threats, and indeed, one of the quintessential Okavango images is of a group of red lechwe running through a haze of kicked-up spray, their chestnut coats glowing in the sunlight. When agitated the lechwe runs with a peculiar gait, holding its head low to the ground and (in the case of males) its long, lyre-shaped horns swept flush to its back, a position thought to prevent the horns from becoming entangled in reeds.

The waterbuck has a similar build to that of the lechwe but it has a shaggy, brownish-grey coat and a distinctive white ring on its rump. The coat contains oils that give it an unmistakable musky odour, a scent that, in some circles, is believed to help reduce predation. Although widespread through Africa, waterbuck occur in fewer numbers in the Delta than one might expect in such an ideal habitat. Much like lechwe, they prefer the floodplain edge, and while they are rarely found far from water they are not as water-dependent as sitatunga and red lechwe and will also graze in open woodlands. Dominant males are territorial and defend their territories by bluff or, if necessary, by fighting, even to the death. Herds of females and young have home ranges that cover several male territories.

Red lechwe ram   *Sitatunga ram*   *Waterbuck cow*

THE LARGER HERBIVORES

A number of large herbivores, including the African buffalo, Burchell's zebra and the blue wildebeest, are locally migrant within the Okavango. Although in the past these animals migrated on a much larger scale, these treks have now stopped, mainly because long lines of 'buffalo fencing' have made their appearance over the last couple of decades (a topic which is discussed in some detail in the Epilogue, pages 167–168). With the recent completion of the Northern Buffalo Fence these migrant animals, along with elephant, are going to find it increasingly difficult to get to the Okavango's feeding grounds. The only avenue offering free passage is to the northeast of the Moremi Game Reserve, into the Chobe National Park.

Although related to domestic cattle, which are generally docile, the African buffalo (*Syncerus caffer*) has gained a reputation as a dangerous animal. Heavily built and bearing an impressive pair of horns, buffalo can become aggressive if cornered or wounded, and will defend members of the herd if they come under attack. They are also highly gregarious creatures, living in herds ranging in size from a few dozen to several thousand, and probably account for the highest biomass in the Okavango region. The permanent population of about 20 000 has in the past been enlarged during the dry season by a substantial influx from the northern regions, but the Northern Buffalo Fence, when completed, is likely to halt the migrations. Buffalo here prefer the

Blue wildebeest herd

Blue wildebeest bull

African buffalo

interior sandveld fringes of larger islands and dry landmasses because these areas provide better grazing than the floodplains during the wet season. They tend not to overgraze an area, and as the grazing gradually deteriorates during the dry season, the herds move closer to water, following the retreating flood. Buffalo are most active at night, when they feed, and at dawn and dusk, when they drink and sometimes graze. From mid-morning till late afternoon they rest in the cover of thickets and tall grass.

Without doubt the best known of Africa's wild horses, the zebra is a gregarious animal, with family groups loosely associating to form large herds. The Okavango is home to Burchell's zebra (*Equus burchelli*), which often mingle with blue wildebeest (*Connochaetes taurinus*), lending safety to both by means of its acute eyesight, hearing and sense of smell. These two species are renowned for their spectacular concentrations and mass migrations in the Serengeti-Mara system, far to the northeast. Although not as numerous in Botswana, both were undoubtedly present in large numbers until the mid-1970s. Zebra and wildebeest used to undertake movements similar to those of the buffalo, but in the last ten years populations of all three groups have dropped dramatically. Estimates are that zebra and buffalo numbers have fallen by approximately 50 percent and the wildebeest count by as much as 80 percent, and it is no accident that this has coincided with a time of intensified fence-building and the expansion of the cattle industry. The wildebeest is well adapted to migration, and even dependent on it, mainly because it needs good grazing and water on a regular basis, and migration allows it access to both new water sources and the best grazing areas (which in turn are better sustained by seasonal exploitation), and also because migration reduces predation. Those wildebeest and zebra that do remain in the Okavango area still embark on mini-migrations, during the wet season, to areas of recent rainfall where the grazing is good. Zebra are the first to enter wet areas, trampling and cropping the tall grasses, and making available the shorter grasses which are the preferred grazing of the wildebeest and the other antelope that follow.

Burchell's zebra

ECOTONE HERBIVORES

On the edges of islands and dry land-masses in the Okavango river system, the ecotone, or transition zone, between woodland and grassland is under constant pressure from herbivores that converge there throughout the year. When the seasonal floods arrive, grazing areas receive some relief as the rising waters inundate the grasslands and prevent animals from feeding here. Following the flood's recession the lush new grasses attract the grazers again, among which are several species of antelope. Also drawn to this ecotone are two browsers, the kudu and the giraffe.

Among the grazers is the tsessebe (*Damaliscus lunatus*). Although this is a relatively sedentary antelope, its diet includes a wide variety of grasses and this has enabled it to thrive in the Okavango region, where it is fairly common. Its dependence on water also makes the Delta an ideal habitat, and the animal never strays far from the water's edge. Despite its ungainly appearance, the tsessebe is reputed to be the fastest antelope in the region. Its long forelegs and sloping back (a build it shares with its relative the wildebeest) enable it to move with a lope that uses far less energy than the rocking gait of other antelope, and it can travel at speed for long distances.

Like the tsessebe, the impala (*Aepyceros melampus*) is relatively sedentary. The woodland/grassland ecotone is perfectly suited to it as it both grazes and browses; the fact that its numbers are healthy throughout southern African is testament to this adaptability. Indeed, the species' success has in places been at the expense of other less adaptable antelope. The impala is a highly gregarious animal, and probably the most abundant antelope in the Okavango. Because of the high concentrations of this antelope in the Okavango, the impala is often disregarded, even though its elegant proportions, attractive reddish-fawn coat and graceful agility make it a pleasure to watch. Bachelor and family herds usually feed in open or light savanna woodland

Sable bull

Giraffe

during the cooler daylight hours, moving into more heavily wooded areas in the heat of the day.

The sable antelope (*Hippotragus niger*) cuts a striking figure against its grassland habitat, the male's glossy black upperparts contrasting with the white of the underparts and face, and its long, ridged horns swept gracefully back. Small herds of sable occur widely throughout the area, but the species is never common, either here or elsewhere in its range. Although seldom a target today, the animal's handsome coat and horns made it an attractive quarry in the heyday of hunting, during the latter years of the nineteenth century. Active mainly at dawn and early evening, the sable antelope nevertheless prefers to drink in the middle of the day in areas where it is undisturbed.

The kudu (*Tragelaphus strepsiceros*) is easily recognised by its large size, the

Impala ram

narrow white stripes on its flanks, and the thin ridge of hair running from head to tail, but it is the bull's spectacular spiralling horns that really set it apart from other antelope. These horns are used in the fights that sometimes occur between rival males during the mating season: the horns are locked in a test of strength, occasionally becoming inextricably entwined and causing the slow death of both animals. The kudu has fairly wide seasonal movement patterns within the Okavango region, dispersing into the woodlands during the wet months then returning to the edge zone in the dry period. The animal also has a fairly catholic diet: predominantly a browser, it prefers the leaves of a wide variety of trees and shrubs, as well as creepers, fruits and pods, but will also eat grass (especially young shoots) and – to the annoyance of farmers – crop plants such as lucerne. Moreover, it is able to eat plants whose sap is toxic and a deterrent to other animals, and when food is scarce it will also chew the bark off trees. In common with the eland, it has powerful hind legs which make it an accomplished jumper, able to clear a 2-metre-high fence without difficulty, and it uses this agility, coupled with its alertness, to escape from danger. Because of their larger size, male kudu have a higher mortality rate than females: the bulkier male is less agile and therefore more susceptible to predation, and its greater food requirements make it more vulnerable when times are hard. One consequence of this is that, in an average herd, there are significantly more females than males. As a primary host of the tsetse fly this antelope, along with others, was hunted heavily in the early parts of this century, but more enlightened programmes are now in place. Although it does succumb to disease it recovers easily, and kudu populations are not in danger.

Sporting an immensely long neck and legs, and a coat pattern worked in jigsaw-piece brown patches on a pale background, the massive giraffe (*Giraffa camelopardalis*) is an unmistakable inhabitant of the Okavango. Common wherever trees occur (most places in the Okavango), it feeds in small, scattered herds from the higher branches, generally favouring acacia during the dry season and mopane and other evergreens during the wet period. Because of its tremendous height – 4,5–5 metres – it feeds on those parts of the tree that are unavailable to other browsers, and with its long, narrow muzzle and prehensile tongue is able to be a highly selective feeder when new shoots, pods and flowers are available. A further advantage conferred by its form is the periscopic view it enjoys over the landscape: giraffes maintain contact with each other and detect danger primarily by sight. If attacked – and the giraffe is a favoured prey of lion and hyaena – it defends itself by kicking with its powerful forelegs. It is most vulnerable when drinking, when its awkward and at times immobilising posture, with forelegs splayed, makes it an easy target. Although social hierarchy is often established peacefully by ritualised 'necking', males sometimes literally come to blows, each swinging his head like a hefty club at his opponent's underbelly.

Kudu bull

Tsessebe

Chacma baboon

THE PRIMATES

Along with impala and lechwe, chacma baboon (*Papio ursinus*) are among the most numerous of the Okavango's mammals, numbering about 250 000. This unmistakable greyish-brown monkey, with its long, dog-like muzzle, is the region's largest primate. Males are up to twice the size of females and sport a mane of longer hair around their neck and shoulders. Baboons are omnivorous animals, foraging during the day in troops of up to a hundred individuals of both sexes. It would seem that such high levels of sociality lower the risk of predation, and baboons are thought to help maintain good relationships within the group by engaging in mutual grooming. Young baboons, and especially stragglers, are vulnerable to many kinds of predator, but the co-operative defence of a troop usually enables them to forage safely in open areas. Some troop members stand guard continually and males will attack potential predators if necessary. Chacma baboons are able to live in a variety of habitats, needing only a supply of water and a safe nocturnal refuge, and as a result they are found throughout the Okavango. Their excellent manual dexterity enables them to forage for a broad range of food and they will even take vertebrate prey when the opportunity presents itself. Within the Delta, lodges and camp-sites fall within their ranges and they will readily 'steal' unattended food. Most adult baboons have the strength to rip open tents so it is advisable to keep all foodstuffs, or anything that resembles them, locked away securely while visiting the area.

The baboon's smaller and less numerous cousin the vervet monkey (*Cercopithecus aethiops*) is also widespread throughout the Delta. Troops are generally not as large as those of baboons, usually numbering around twenty animals. Whereas the baboon is at home in open areas, the vervet monkey finds safety in the tree canopy, and although it is regarded as a forest edge specialist it rarely forages far from cover, leaving the canopy only

Chacma baboon

to drink – and warily at that. Its size and foraging habits make it more vulnerable to predation than other primates, and perhaps because of this it has developed a relatively sophisticated system of alarm calls. Specific to the type of predator encountered, these calls are thought to be significant for the light they shed on the evolution of language. Like other primates, vervet monkeys are omnivorous, their manual dexterity enabling them to forage expertly for the most readily available food.

The Okavango's only other primate is the lesser bushbaby (*Galago moholi*). Restricted to woodland areas and totally nocturnal, this animal is well suited to its habitat: it has the strength to leap a distance of up to 5 metres between trees, can manoeuvre itself in the air with the help of its long, rudder-like tail, and both its ability to grasp and the cushioning afforded by its thick fur enable it to come to rest in the branches of thorn trees. The latter ability is also an important factor in its survival: within the spiky protection of dense thorn trees this little primate can remain safe, undisturbed by raptors and other predators. It sleeps in small family groups during the day before venturing out by moonlight to forage alone. Specially adapted lower teeth enable this animal to gather tree gum, its primary food source, though it also eats insects, which it detects with its highly mobile ears.

Lesser bushbaby

Vervet monkey

Lioness

THE CARNIVORES

The big cats are undoubtedly the main drawcard of Africa's wildlife sanctuaries, and visitors to the Okavango Delta are fortunate in that, because there are large numbers of ungulates here, the area supports sizeable populations of all the major African carnivores. The lion and spotted hyaena are probably the most obvious of these residents, and lion are likely be seen on any safari to the Okavango, though sightings of the other two big cats, the leopard and the cheetah, are not as common. The relationship between the predators and their prey is an interesting one. Population sizes on both sides of the equation are affected by the success of the other: not only do the predators keep populations of prey animals in check, but the availability of prey is a good indicator of the state of the predator populations. Moreover, lion and other predators tend to take the 'easy pickings' from herds of some species – the sick, the old and the very young – thereby leaving the strongest and healthiest animals to perpetuate the species.

Lion (*Panthera leo*) are found throughout the Delta's dryland areas and larger islands, but their presence is quite

Lion cub

unpredictable. Surprisingly, the lions of the Okavango will readily enter water to reach islands or cross floodplains. The prides within the Delta display marked dietary preferences, with some specialising in taking particular animal species. The patterns of prey distribution change markedly over the seasons as the herbivores migrate over considerable distances according to local food and water conditions, and in response to this lions move extensively within their territories, following prey. Concealing themselves amidst vegetation, they stalk their prey under cover of darkness, giving chase only for the last couple of hundred metres. Contrary to what might be expected, lion are opportunistic feeders and often scavenge kills from smaller predators. Although they will drink if given the opportunity, they derive most of their moisture requirements from their prey so a source of water is not a habitat requirement. Lion are the most sociable of the big cats, normally associating in prides which comprise a number of related females and their offspring. The females and cubs fall under the dominance of a single pride male or, more usually, a coalition of related males. These animals are primarily nocturnal, and the roars of resident prides are a constant feature of the Okavango night. Consequently, unless encountered very early in the morning, they are most frequently seen sleeping.

Lioness and lion

Often described as the most beautiful of Africa's big cats, the leopard *(Panthera pardus)* is able to live in many types of habitat and is found throughout the Okavango. Its golden coat, dotted with black rosettes, provides a highly effective camouflage and this, together with the animal's cunning, makes it an elusive creature. In the more popular safari areas, though, it is seen quite often and has no doubt become accustomed to the presence of humans and vehicles. Unless a female has young cubs, leopard are generally seen alone. Their preferred habitats are woodland and forested islands, as these provide the necessary cover for stalking and ambushing prey at close range. Prey consists mainly of small to medium-sized antelope, and this cat will also eat a variety of other small creatures, although, contrary to popular belief, the baboon barely features on its menu! The leopard will stalk its prey patiently, eventually pouncing on it from as close a range as possible and biting its throat to asphyxiate it. It will sometimes hoist the kill into a tree to keep it out of the reach of scavengers, and will also climb to escape predators and, occasionally, to rest, but otherwise it stays on the ground. Both male and female leopards defend individual territories against others of their sex.

The Okavango's other spotted big cat is the cheetah *(Acinonyx jubatus)* which, because of the way it hunts – relying on a high-speed chase to catch its prey – tends to stay close to floodplains and other open areas. It does, however, need patches of scrub for cover, both for stalking and for hiding its prey. With its deep chest, streamlined body and long tail the cheetah is built for speed. But although it is capable of chasing prey at speeds of up to 100 kilometres per hour over short distances, the exertion required for this feat is so great that the cheetah must rest before starting to feed; furthermore, this cat lacks sufficient body strength to match most other large predators, and for these two reasons alone its kills are often pirated by other predators. To reduce the risk of this happening the cheetah hunts almost exclusively during the day, when the majority of other predators are inactive. Like most other cats, cheetah are solitary except when raising young, although males sometimes form lifelong coalitions. Only males maintain any sort of territory. At some stage in its history, the cheetah reached the brink of extinction and consequently today's cheetah populations display almost no genetic diversity. This makes these animals especially susceptible to disease and reproductive afflictions, such

Leopard

Leopard

Cheetah

as abnormal sperm and reduced birth rates. Although ideal cheetah habitat is in plentiful supply in the Okavango, the animal is inexplicably uncommon in the region. Once vulnerable to hunters because of its much prized spotted coat, it is now protected virtually throughout its range.

The Okavango is also home to several other large predators, including hyaena, jackal and wild dog.

The spotted hyaena (*Crocuta crocuta*) occurs widely throughout the Okavango, and together with the roar of the lion, its cackle and long, drawn-out whoop contribute to the area's symphony of familiar nocturnal sounds. Although in the past this animal was perceived as little more than a cowardly scavenger lurking around the edges of other predators' kills, it does not in fact scavenge any more than the much revered lion. Indeed, it is a capable killer in its own right, able to give chase at speeds of up to 60 kilometres per hour over a distance of 3 kilometres or more. Far from being a coward, it is also a plucky fighter when it needs to be, and will stand up to lions if they interfere with its meal, mobbing them if necessary. Much of the spotted hyaena's success is due to its adaptability: it has a varied diet, and this, combined with opportunistic behaviour, gives it great scope for obtaining food. It will hunt alone or in packs, scavenge or bring down its own kill, take what is left lying around after another predator's meal or fight off other animals before they have had their fill. Furthermore, its powerful jaws enable it to crunch up bones and obtain the rich nutrients or the bone marrow unavailable to many other carnivores. In the Okavango the spotted hyaena, like its rival the lion, will regularly swim across water to follow its prey. Unlike in most other mammal species, the female is dominant in the clan, with even the lowest-ranking female taking precedence over the highest-ranking male. To the casual observer the sexes may be difficult to distinguish, as their external genital organs are similar in appearance, and in fact levels of male hormones in the

Spotted hyaena

African wild dog

female are high. Female dominance is important for the survival of the species: the cubs are dependent on their mother's milk for nine to twelve months, so she must be able to eat and return to the den quickly to suckle them. Aggression in the den runs high, and sibling rivalry between cubs can sometimes lead to siblicide, especially if the cubs are sisters. Although its relative the brown hyaena (*Hyaena brunnea*) also occurs in the Delta region, this species is more widespread in the Kalahari sandveld to the west and south of the Delta, and is seldom seen here.

Along with South Africa's Kruger National Park and Tanzania's Selous Game Reserve, the Okavango Delta is home to one of the few remaining viable populations of Africa's most endangered carnivore, the African wild dog (*Lycaon pictus*) – one which holds the dubious honour of being the largest unprotected wild dog population still in existence. Though it is an efficient hunter, regularly produces sizeable litters of puppies and can live in large packs with a minimum of strife, the wild dog's survival is curtailed by factors such as disease (including rabies and distemper) and predation by lion. Pups are usually produced by the alpha pair in a pack, with the other members of the pack helping to raise and protect them. For the first three months of the pups' life the pack's range is drastically reduced, with hunting expeditions being mounted twice a day from the den area. For the most part, however, the wild dog moves over a very large range, especially if its prey is migratory. Like the spotted hyaena, it is a courser, chasing down its prey relentlessly and with incredible stamina until the exhausted quarry is taken. The reputation of the wild dog as a ruthless and wanton destroyer is probably directly related to the fact that it kills in packs, and to the seemingly gruesome way in which it dispatches its prey – by disembowelment – though this is in fact by far the quickest method of killing of any used by the large carnivores. In the competition for prey, lion will almost invariably win the day, to the extent that in some places wild dog try to avoid lion country. On the other hand, unless it is significantly out-numbered, the wild dog will usually get the upper hand over the spotted hyaena when these two compete for food. In the Okavango, lion regularly expropriate kills from wild dogs and seem to go out of their way to attempt to kill them. Researchers feel that there is no apparent reason for lion to display such enmity towards wild dogs, and go so far as to suggest that these dogs live in packs primarily to prevent lion predation.

Another member of the dog family, the jackal, is represented by two species in the Delta. With its silver-grey back and tan to white underside, the black-backed jackal (*Canis mesomelas*) is a handsome animal, but one that has been ruthlessly persecuted on Africa's farmlands because of its predilection for small stock. Nevertheless it is one of the most successful of carnivores, occurring widely throughout southern Africa in all habitat types. Its success in the Okavango is due to its adaptability and catholic diet: it will eat almost any edible material it finds. The black-blacked jackal is one of the few mammals that take a mate for life, yet its social system is more complex than the simple family unit. Family groups act co-operatively, liaising and forming temporary packs when this is expedient. Operating as a pack, jackal can find widely distributed food resources and avoid predation by communicating with each other over some distance.

The Moremi Game Reserve is one of the prime sites in Africa to see the black-backed jackal's cousin, the side-striped jackal (*Canis adustus*). This animal is slightly more heavily built than its cousin and has a faint white stripe running down each flank. It is just as versatile, though in the region relies mostly on scavenged meat and rodents for food. Research in Zimbabwe has shown that it will eat certain berries, when they are ripe, to the exclusion of all other food. The species is more likely to be seen in seasonally flooded areas than in woodlands, and is more water-dependent than the black-backed jackal.

Black-backed jackal cub

Side-striped jackal cubs

Reed cormorant

BIRDS

The Okavango Delta system is home to a wealth of bird species. Prime bird-watching areas are those with a mix of habitats such as the Panhandle, the seasonal Delta and the parts of the Moremi Game Reserve that are close to water. Birdlife in the permanent Delta is not as prolific as in these other regions since the water is usually too deep for waders. There are more than 400 bird species present in the Okavango ecosystem, so it is impossible to introduce or illustrate anything like the complete range. Those that follow have been chosen because they are either the most regularly encountered or the most representative of the Okavango's avian inhabitants.

AQUATIC BIRDS

These birds remain permanently close to water and comprise the extended pelican family (pelicans, darters and cormorants) together with ducks and geese. They occur throughout the Okavango region and are often seen, although nowhere are they prolific.

The reed cormorant (*Phalacrocorax africanus*) and the darter (*Anhinga rufa*) are somewhat similar in appearance, but the latter can be identified by its longer, thinner neck and straight, sharp beak, while the reed cormorant's beak is shorter and slightly hooked. The darter is often seen on the region's waterways with only its neck protruding above the water, often held in an S-bend, and for this reason it has acquired its local name, 'snakebird'.

Fish dominate the diet of a number of birds in the Delta, and fishing techniques are many and varied among the region's aquatic birds – the reed cormorant and darter, for instance, enter the prey's domain, beneath the water surface. By virtue of the bend in the darter's neck, this bird can 'harpoon' its prey with its rapier-like bill (earning it its common English name). The reed cormorant, on the other hand, pursues its prey underwater; unlike marine reed cormorants which must sometimes dive to depths of up to 100 metres to feed, inland birds rarely need to venture more than 6 metres underwater to secure a meal.

The plumage of both species is very absorbent, and it is assumed that because the feathers become easily waterlogged the bird's buoyancy is reduced and it can dive with greater freedom than if its plumage were waterproof. Individuals are often seen on perches near or over the water, with their wings spread – an aid both to the drying out process and, it is thought, to their digestion as well. In the Delta, cormorants make their nests in the islands that often develop around water fig trees.

Darter

White pelicans

Both the white pelican (*Pelecanus onocrotalus*) and the pink-backed pelican (*P. rufescens*) are found throughout the Okavango. Normally they occur in sizeable mixed flocks, although the two species forage separately. The pink-backed pelican is noticeably smaller and greyer than its white relative, and in flight the latter's wings have black trailing edges. The pelican's expandable pouch is used not (as is popularly believed) to store or carry fish, but as a scoop when foraging. The occurrence of these nomadic birds is dictated largely by the availability of food, and flocks will fly considerable distances over the subcontinent to find profitable foraging. Their presence in the Delta is some-what erratic – a drying pan that hosts a flock of a hundred pelicans one day might be deserted the next – though their favoured breeding ground is the Makgadikgadi Pans.

Egyptian geese

Fourteen of the sixteen duck and goose species found in southern Africa are listed as occurring in the Okavango. For what appears to be an ideal habitat for the Anatidae, this family is poorly represented in the Delta, and surprisingly, only five or six of these species are seen regularly. Among these are three 'perching' birds: the spur-winged goose (*Plectropterus gambensis*), the pygmy goose (*Nettapus auritus*) and the knob-billed duck (*Sarkidiornis melanotos*). All will occasionally use a tree to perch in, a bizarre sight in the case of the huge spur-winged goose. Both the knob-billed duck and the pygmy goose breed in hollows in tree trunks, sites which are provided in abundance by the region's countless mopane trees. Although it has a goose-like head and neck, the delicate pygmy goose is in fact not a goose at all, but a duck. The population density of the pygmy goose in the Okavango is higher than almost anywhere else in its range, probably because of the abundance of waterlilies, the bird's favourite food. It is easily disturbed, however, and is most likely to be seen when flying away.

White-faced ducks

As ubiquitous here as in all other southern African waterways is the Egyptian goose (*Alopochen aegyptiacus*). During the breeding season noisy gatherings of the bird can be seen throughout the Delta, with the males boisterously chasing intruders from their territories. All three species of 'whistling duck' – the white-faced duck (*Dendrocygna viduata*), the fulvous duck (*D. bicolor*) and the white-backed duck (*Thalassornis leuconotus*) – are represented in the Delta. The most abundant of the three is the white-faced duck; although commonly found on the more open waters of the Delta it is sensitive to human presence. When disturbed it flies off uttering its trisyllabic whistle, the flock circling until it finds an undisturbed area.

Knob-billed duck

Cattle egret

Three-banded plover

Grey heron

BIRDS OF THE WATER'S EDGE

The Okavango system's numerous sandbanks, shorelines, rafts of aquatic vegetation and areas of shallow water provide ideal habitats for birds that live at the water's edge, a group characterised by a mix of long legs, long toes and ingenious hunting techniques.

Like the darters, cormorants and pelicans, the Ardeidae (herons and egrets) is a mainly fish-eating family whose bills, legs and necks are long relative to their body size. Eighteen of the world's 62 heron species live in the Delta, and range in size from the dwarf bittern (*Ixobrychus sturmii*) at 25 centimetres in length to the goliath heron (*Ardea goliath*) at 140 centimetres. With the abundance of fish in the Delta region, this area is particularly suitable for herons and storks, all of which rely on fish for a large proportion of their diet. These two families occur throughout the permanent Delta and its floodplains. The floodplains are particularly favoured when they have been recently inundated, at which time they attract large numbers of fish in search of feeding and breeding grounds. Each species employs unique fishing methods, ranging from stalking in the shallows to the sophisticated umbrella method used by the black egret (*Egretta ardesiaca*) (see also pages 140–141 and 143). Much competition exists between members of this group for prime fishing spots, and a clear pecking order has been established. This is constantly reinforced by apparently ritualised chases that occur between bouts of feeding. Other birds also take advantage of the prodigious talent the Ardeidae have for hunting: pelicans and fish eagles regularly attempt to 'pirate' catches from them, their success depending largely on the size of the chosen victim. Some of the storks, though, prefer foraging in the surrounding savanna areas, where they often stalk prey along the water's edge. Preferences vary from species to species but generally include small mammals, reptiles, insects, amphibians and even other birds.

Storks, herons and egrets are the most numerous inhabitants of the communal nesting sites that are found in water fig thickets in lagoons throughout the Delta. These birds begin breeding towards the end of the dry season, when the receding waters of the floodplains provide a ready larder of trapped fish for their new chicks. Breeding alongside many other species in the fig trees is the slaty egret (*Egretta vinaceigula*), one of the world's rarest herons: it is largely confined to and breeds solely in the Okavango. Recognised as a valid

African jacana

African skimmers

species as recently as 1971, little is known about the limited distribution and breeding habits of this bird, except that its future is precariously linked to that of the Delta.

The Okavango system is also an important breeding ground for the rufous-bellied heron (*Ardeola rufiventris*), marabou stork (*Leptoptilos crumeniferus*) and yellow-billed stork (*Mycteria ibis*), all active participants in Delta life. For the yellow-billed stork in particular, listed as rare in a recent assessment of southern Africa's endangered birds, the Delta is the primary breeding ground in the region.

The Rallidae family includes the rails, crakes, coots and gallinules – a collection of similarly built birds whose long toes enable them to walk on aquatic vegetation. Because of this adaptation the Okavango provides a particularly suitable environment for the family. With the exception of the gallinules and coots, they are generally secretive, wary birds and are only seen when they leave the cover of waterside reedbeds. They are confined largely to areas of permanent water where, it is thought, their narrow bodies help them to push their way through thick vegetation. On the other hand, purple gallinules (*Porphyrio porphyrio*) and red-knobbed coots (*Fulica cristata*), in the words of one authority, 'let it all hang out'. Blessed with an iridescent plumage, purple gallinules are noisy birds that often rob the nests of other birds and generate enormous amounts of litter when feeding on plants, rightfully deserving their reputation as the 'thugs' of the marshland bird community.

Little bittern

The conspicuous and perky African jacana (*Actophilornis africanus*) is similar in appearance to the birds of the Rallidae family, and takes its behavioural cues from the purple gallinule. It has even longer toes – longer, proportionately, than those of any other bird species – and is commonly seen walking across waterlily leaves or flying around in small, noisy groups, absorbed in territorial struggles. The African jacana is a polyandrous species – that is, the female usually has more than one male partner. The male is solely responsible for brooding and raising the chicks and receives no assistance at all from the female. The latter can be almost twice the size of her mate and as a result has slightly more difficulty moving across floating vegetation. The immature bird is often confused with the smaller lesser jacana (*Microparra capensis*), a drab and less bombastic relative; the best way to tell them apart is by the white lining to the trailing edge of the lesser jacana's wing, and by its rufous, rather than dark brown, crown.

Most prominent of the Okavango's shorebirds are members of the plover family (Charadriidae). The three-banded plover (*Charadrius tricollaris*) and blacksmith plover (*Vanellus armatus*) both forage along and nest near the water's edge. Plovers are renowned in popular culture as birds that protect their nests from all potential threats, however big. Like the African jacana, the uncommon long-toed plover (*V. crassirostris*) prefers to feed from floating vegetation, eating insects which it disturbs by shaking lily leaves and other aquatic vegetation with its feet. Although similar in build to the blacksmith plover, it does not tolerate the presence of the latter, more common bird and often 'dive-bombs' it.

Saddle-billed stork

The African skimmer (*Rhynchops flavirostris*) is one of the most distinctive birds of the Delta region, though far from common. Its bold black and white markings and its prominent red bill, with the lower mandible longer than the upper, render it unmistakable. This bird's feeding method is unique: it flies low over the water with its long lower mandible just breaking the water's surface, and as soon as the mandible touches anything edible it snaps shut (see contents page). An intra-African migrant, the skimmer arrives in the Okavango in autumn and breeds from July to December, building its nest in a shallow scrape on the exposed sandbanks of the Panhandle and in some of the smaller pans of the dryland areas. Sadly, massive areas of similar sandbanks have been lost through dam-building in the rest of southern Africa, most notably on the Zambezi River, making the species vulnerable. The construction of dams causes previously available sandbanks to be flooded, and dam walls trap sediment, preventing further sandbanks from forming downstream. Conservation programmes are in place to educate users of the Okavango system about the dangers the African skimmer faces; bow waves from motorboats that wash over their nests and disturbance and trampling inflicted by clumsy people are just some of the risks to which this bird is subject.

Marabou stork

African hawk eagle

BIRDS OF PREY

A wide variety of raptors make their home in the Okavango, though these birds are by and large not as evident here as they are in other southern African game sanctuaries. In dryland areas vultures are probably the most visible birds of prey, though the thickly wooded terrain makes for less than ideal viewing conditions. A notable exception is the Khwai area of Moremi Game Reserve where, during the drier months, large concentrations of eagles occur. Most remarkable of these are the groups of immature bateleurs (*Terathopius ecaudatus*) and tawny

African fish eagle

Pel's fishing owl

eagles (*Aquila rapax*) that loiter at the drying ends of the river to drink, bathe and hunt the flocks of doves that emerge from the surrounding woodlands to drink.

By far the most visible species in the wetlands is the African fish eagle, and the least evident is the nocturnal Pel's fishing owl. While the lion's roar and the hyaena's whoop dominate the sounds of dryland Okavango, the distinctive, haunting calls of the fish eagle and the fishing owl epitomise the waterways.

Pairs of fish eagle (*Haliaeetus vocifer*) are commonly seen along all the region's waterways. They occupy fairly static and small territories centred on their nest sites. Although fairly territorial in the breeding season, fish eagles are sometimes seen in large numbers, oblivious to territorial imperatives, in newly flooded areas and around drying pools. This raptor is easily seen: safari operators in the Okavango habitually feed them, and as a result they will readily swoop down to catch the fish thrown to them.

The large, ginger-coloured Pel's fishing owl (*Scotopelia peli*) is far more elusive. Totally nocturnal, it spends the daylight hours in thickly forested areas but is easily put to flight. By night it hunts from regular perches that overhang prime fishing spots along the waterways. Depending on the particular area, densities of the fishing owl may be as high as one pair for every kilometre of waterfront. The best chance of seeing one is from a boat in the Panhandle, at night, with the use of a spotlight.

Barred owl

Hooded vultures

Carmine bee-eaters

MIXED-HABITAT BIRDS

Among the birds commonly found around both the aquatic and dryland habitats of the Okavango are kingfishers (Alcedinidae) and bee-eaters (Meropidae). The pied kingfisher (*Ceryle rudis*) is abundant in the Okavango and is often seen hovering over a channel before diving into the water to retrieve a fish. The beautifully iridescent malachite kingfisher (*Alcedo cristata*) prefers to hunt small fish from a perch overhanging the water's edge. Despite their common name, not all kingfishers eat fish: the woodland kingfisher (*Halcyon senegalensis*) – a summer migrant from Central Africa – and the brown-hooded kingfisher (*H. albiventris*) both prefer the dryland areas and eat mainly insects, while the giant kingfisher (*C. maxima*), though it will take fish from time to time, subsists mainly on crabs.

Bee-eaters are found in great numbers in the Delta, especially when the ranks of the resident white-fronted, swallow-tailed and little bee-eaters (*Merops bullockoides*, *M. hirundineus* and *M. pusillus*) are swollen by the arrival of a number of migrant species, including carmine, European and blue-cheeked bee-eaters (*M. nubicoides*, *M. apiaster* and *M. persicus*), in August and September. Though these birds will take a range of insects, they have gained their name from the preference some show for bees, and their ability to

Little bee-eater

Malachite kingfisher

Pied kingfisher

Giant kingfisher

White-fronted bee-eaters

Woodland kingfisher

Lilac-breasted roller

wipe the sting off the tail of a bee before consuming it. The white-fronted bee-eater and carmine bee-eater hawk insects in flight over both dry land and water, often dispersing into the surrounding areas to forage. Both species nest in the steep sandbanks of the Panhandle, often tunnelling deep into the bank to lay their eggs. On rare occasions carmine bee-eaters will build their nests on flat ground and several of these sites can be visited in the region; indeed, the carmine bee-eater's breeding colonies in the Panhandle are among the more striking spectacles of the Okavango. Several hundred of these boldly coloured birds fly to and from their sandbank burrows, uttering their strange high-pitched calls. Little bee-eaters and swallow-tailed bee-eaters prefer woodland habitats, and nest in sandbanks – and sometimes in abandoned termite mounds – away from water.

DRYLAND BIRDS

Francolin and hornbills are probably the most commonly seen (and heard) of the Okavango's dryland birds. Anyone visiting the region is likely to be woken at some stage by the harsh, insistent cackling of a francolin, and sometimes one has to swerve as they dart in front of one's vehicle, running along in the tracks and only taking to flight at the last possible moment! Wherever there is a termite mound, it is likely to be topped by one of these birds standing sentinel. The red-billed francolin (*Francolinus adspersus*), Swainson's francolin (*F. swainsonii*) and the crested francolin (*F. sephaena*) are the most commonly encountered species. From a distance all three appear dull brown but closer inspection reveals differences in their cryptic coloration and markings. Males can be distinguished from females by the spurs on their legs which they use in territorial defence. Francolins are commonly seen foraging in small groups in the dryland areas.

The helmeted guineafowl (*Numida meleagris*), which belongs to a related family, is a familiar sight throughout the dryland areas of the Delta, though it is more numerous northeast of here. It is a highly gregarious bird and, with its white-spotted black body and the bare blue and red skin on its head, it is quite unmistakable. It is usually seen on the edge of mopane woodland, foraging on the ground for insects and seeds or making its way down to water to drink.

The hornbills are a collection of large birds characterised by their disproportionately large, heavy beaks, sometimes with a casque. A number of species commonly occur in the dryland areas. The smaller hornbills are mostly omnivorous, sometimes feeding on fruit and other times on insects, especially winged termites, and smaller vertebrates like frogs and rodents. The large, terrestrial ground hornbill (*Bucorvus leadbeateri*) subsists mostly on small animals, particularly rodents and reptiles. The yellow-billed hornbill (*Tockus leucomelas*) is particularly abundant, and is often found feeding in the road. In summer, puddles in vehicle tracks also provide a good source of the mud which the bird uses in the construction of its nest. In most hornbill species the female seals herself into the nest with mud brought by the male, leaving only a small slit through which the male feeds her. Once inside, she moults and lines the nest with her own feathers. The similar-sized red-billed hornbill (*T. erythrorhynchus*), grey hornbill (*T. nasutus*) and Bradfield's hornbill (*T. bradfieldi*) also occur in the region.

Other very common dryland birds, drawn to the area by the abundance of mopane woodland, are Arnot's chat and a number of starling species. Arnot's chat (*Thamnolaea arnoti*) is another hole-nesting creature hosted by the Delta's extensive mopane woodlands. It is a diminutive black and white bird which is commonly seen in small, widely spread groups, perching at low levels or foraging for insects on the woodland floor.

Starlings are among the most successful bird species in the world. Three of the family's members are especially visible in the Delta region: the greater blue-eared starling (*Lamprotornis chalybaeus*), Burchell's starling (*L. australis*) and the long-tailed starling (*L. mevesii*). All three have very similar glossy, blue-green bodies which contrast attractively with the lighter greens and oranges of their surroundings. Their constant bubbling calls are a typical sound of the mopane woodlands.

Burchell's starling

Helmeted guineafowl

Swainson's francolin

Red-billed hornbill

Painted reed frog

Water monitor lizard

Spotted bush snake

Nile crocodile

REPTILES AND AMPHIBIANS

The most evident of the Okavango's reptiles is the Nile crocodile (*Crocodylus niloticus*). Present in most of the Delta's waterways, it occurs in large concentrations only in the Panhandle, its preferred breeding site. The sandbanks where crocodiles lay their eggs form throughout the area between September and January, when water levels are lower. Large individuals are often seen splashing into the water when disturbed, but like other reptiles crocodiles are quite retiring creatures, possibly as a result of hunting pressure in earlier years. Intense commercial hunting operations in the 1950s and 1960s, undertaken largely for its much prized skin, resulted in the slaughter of tens of thousands of the animals, and the crocodile population declined substantially. Given their long life span, the older reptiles are probably wary of humans. One of the most prolific of hunters of that time, John Seaman, later set up a crocodile-breeding farm near Maun and so became instrumental in replenishing the crocodile population he initially helped to deplete: to keep the population stable, commercial breeders have to return 5 percent of all hatchlings to the waterways – an effective measure, as the Okavango's crocodile numbers are on the rise once again.

Large monitor lizards and a variety of much smaller geckos and lizards are found throughout the dry and wetland habitats. Shelled reptiles – terrapins and tortoises – are also well represented, the former favouring wetter regions and the latter dry land.

A number of snakes, too, take their place in this wetland wilderness, and while most are harmless there are several venomous and some potentially lethal varieties, not least of all the black mamba, whose venom is highly toxic. Like most other snakes, however, it will retreat readily if allowed to do so and will only strike if disturbed suddenly or provoked. A snake's presence is often indicated by noisy gatherings of squirrels and birds. Possibly because of the threat snakes pose to their nests, mixed flocks of birds often congregate to mob these reptiles until they leave the area.

In most areas bordering waterways or marshy areas the competing voices of a multitude of frogs provide a nocturnal serenade. They are possibly the most numerous animals in the grasslands and adjacent wetlands, and several species are found in the Delta. The most spectacular is the painted reed frog (*Hyperolius marmoratus*), a tiny, very colourful individual which occurs in a variety of forms. Its limbs are specially adapted, with flattened discs on the toes enabling it to climb slippery surfaces, such as the stems of the reeds that proliferate throughout its range. Many predatory birds prey voraciously on these frogs throughout the summer months, when they are most active and at their most abundant.

INVERTEBRATES

As in many other places on the planet, vast numbers of largely unnoticed invertebrates inhabit the Okavango region and could in themselves be the subject of an entire book. Three of these, however, have played a significant part in the formation and continued existence of the system and are worthy of mention.

Owing to its effect on the very structure of the area itself, the termite is undoubtedly the most noteworthy. Although many termite species inhabit the Kalahari and Okavango regions, the most evident – largely because of the conspicuous mounds, or termitaria, it creates – is the fungus termite (*Macrotermes michaelseni*). These termite mounds are constructed from clay, sand and saliva, and form the basis of many of the numerous islands that dot the Delta. Termites are mostly nocturnal, emerging after dark to forage. The damp patches often seen on the sides of active termitaria in the early morning are evidence of the constant enlarging and metamorphosis of the mounds.

As harbingers of disease, mosquitoes and tsetse fly (*Glossina morsitans*) have saved the Okavango Delta from human depredations for some time. The tsetse fly carries the trypanosome parasite that causes sleeping sickness in humans and nagama in cattle. Its presence in the Delta long served as a natural barrier to people and their cattle attempting to encroach on the area. Stories recounted by early visitors to the region are littered with references to the bites of the fly. Early attempts to eradicate the tsetse fly were mostly misguided and focused on its perceived hosts. Game and trees, because they provided the fly with food and cover, were targeted in destructive campaigns that failed to make an impact on the fly's populations, but over 50 000 animals and vast areas of bush were destroyed. Subsequent eradication efforts have turned to the controversial spraying of insecticides and erection of chemical traps. Although these attempts have failed to eradicate the tsetse fly, its distribution is now severely curtailed and the fly is no longer a health threat. The guardianship that it provided to the Okavango's wildlife, however, is lost, and ironically the much loathed buffalo fences at present constitute one of the main barriers keeping humans and their cattle out of the pristine Delta areas.

An almost constant nocturnal attendant in the Okavango is the mosquito, and the threat of malaria is very real. The malaria parasite *Plasmodium* is transmitted only by the female of the *Anopheles* mosquito. Surprisingly, mosquitoes normally subsist on plant sap, but the female mosquito has to feed on animal blood to provide her with the necessary protein to lay eggs; this she does at a rate of about a hundred eggs every four days. In recent times the *Plasmodium* parasite has become problematic again as it has developed increasing degrees of immunity to traditional malaria antidotes.

The Delta is also home to a spectacular array of less threatening invertebrates. Ants, beetles, dragonflies, butterflies, damselflies and ordinary irritating flies are everywhere. Spiders, ticks, crabs and scorpions are equally well represented, although densities, especially of scorpions, are lower here than in the surrounding Kalahari region.

Emperor moth caterpillars

Stick insect

Orb-web spider

Dragonfly

Termite mound

The Performance

Actions and interactions

Τhe Okavango is one of the last substantial wetland areas left on Earth. Against this spectacular backdrop the cast of creatures great and small play out the daily drama of their lives, in constant interaction with each other and with their environment, while the seasonal rhythm of its waters provides the tempo that guides their behaviour from one end of the year to the other.

Animals in the Okavango Delta, like those in other wilderness areas across the planet, are primarily concerned with three things: procreation, eating and drinking enough to keep themselves alive, and protecting themselves. They also take time out to sleep and play. Although the methods used to engage in these activities differ from species to species, and although some animals may spend more time on one task than another, the basic objectives remain the same. The result is a vast array of behaviours, the permutations of which are endless: the themes are repeated year after year, but the details are never the same, the events never monotonous.

The photographs that follow are a record of one such year – a chronicle of the lives of the animals that play out their roles in the Okavango's wilderness theatre.

Pied kingfisher

Saddle-billed storks and secretarybird

Zebra mare and foal

SOCIALITY, TERRITORIALITY AND BREEDING

On an evolutionary level, an animal's proficiency is measured by its reproductive success. All other activities it performs are geared towards ensuring that the individual has the best possible chance of passing on its genes to future generations. To achieve this, animals need to do several things: they must establish a hierarchy within their species, and either individually or as members of a group they must define a territory, find a mate, and successfully raise offspring by providing them with sufficient food, shelter and safety to reach adulthood.

Some animals manage this by forming a group. Being part of a flock, herd, pack or pride entails several membership benefits: finding food and a mate is easier, and the risk of predation reduced. More eyes mean a better defence system, and although groups are still preyed on, the probability of any individual being the victim is substantially less than if it were alone. Groups also lessen the need for all members of a species to procreate: sometimes a subordinate stands a better chance of passing on its genes by helping a close relative (a large proportion of whose genetic material is shared) to rear young than by finding a mate; in this way it contributes indirectly to the procreation of its own lineage.

Different social systems exist throughout the animal kingdom. The most advanced forms of sociality occur in mammalian society, with primates, elephants and large social predators like lions and wild dogs having the most complex relationships. Social bonds are often established and maintained through extensive grooming sessions, especially common in baboons and monkeys, some mongooses and the social carnivores. The

Okavango is home to several gregarious animals. Baboon troops containing as many as a hundred individuals range over much of the Delta and, in company with buffalo, probably account for its highest biomass, while red-billed queleas (*Quelea quelea*) can literally block out the sunlight with their massed flocks numbering up to 100 000 birds.

Most animals maintain territories (exclusively occupied and actively demarcated areas) or home ranges (areas which the animal frequents). Establishing and maintaining a territory is usually the concern of adult males, although females of some species, mainly overtly matriarchal species such as spotted hyaena, do maintain their own territories. Mature females rarely stray far from their natal range; because of this, females that come into contact with each other tend to be related, and there is potentially less aggression between them. Some territories are permanent while others, like those of animals that are involved in regular migrations, are temporary. The maintenance of a territory entitles an animal to the use of its resources, including food and the services of subordinate animals of the same species. Such animals typically help to hunt and defend the territory, and are also a source of potential mates. Only the strongest and fittest animals are able to maintain territories and gain access to breeding opportunities, and consequently only the best genes are passed on to future generations. Territories are maintained mainly through advertising by sight, smell and sound. Such displays, if respected, reduce the potential of aggression among animals of the same species. Most animal sounds heard in the Okavango, like the call of a pair of fish eagles or a lion's roar, are used for this purpose. Only when an animal is intent on challenging for a territory do violent clashes occur. Individuals that do not manage to establish a territory form non-breeding reserves and often create bachelor groups.

The quest to breed successfully has resulted in an amazing line-up of breeding strategies, several of which can be observed in the Okavango. Different bird species, for instance, employ different strategies. Larger, longer-living birds, including many raptors, tend to invest heavily in raising a single chick, whereas many smaller birds exercise less parental care and to compensate lay bigger clutches of eggs – of which only some will hatch and even fewer produce chicks that will survive to adulthood. As the young of most species feature prominently in the diet of predators, the tactic of inundating the region's predators with potential prey is employed by many species. Insects and reptiles produce large (sometimes vast) numbers of offspring, and antelope co-ordinate their delivery times so that the young of a species are all born within a relatively short space of time; with so many young around, predators cannot possibly kill all the juveniles, and some inevitably survive infancy.

Parental care also differs markedly from species to species. Some young need to be looked after for a long time after birth, while antelope, for instance, normally start walking within minutes of being born and can keep up with a running herd soon afterwards. Some species choose to give birth in burrows that offer protection to their offspring; others, like the lions of the Okavango, move to the relative seclusion of islands or thickets to give birth. During their late-winter breeding season large numbers of storks and herons gather in communal nesting sites on water fig tree islands in the Delta's lagoons, which afford them better protection from land-based predators. A few birds, such as the African skimmer, nest openly on sandbanks and are particularly vulnerable to disturbance by man and the attentions of numerous predators. A tactic for which cuckoos are renowned is to ignore totally the responsibilities of parenthood: these birds lay their eggs in other birds' nests, and the chicks are raised entirely by the gullible foster parents.

Little bee-eaters

Spotted hyaena cubs

Impala

ANIMAL COMMUNITIES

On the edge of a floodplain in Santawani, south of Moremi Game Reserve, a herd of female impala, alerted by the alarm snort given by one of their number, stare intently at a passing hyaena. Because impala are the most prevalent antelope species in most parts of the Okavango, they are also the most commonly preyed upon, and some biologists suggest that the primary reason impala form herds is to reduce this risk of predation. They are territorial antelope and form single-sex herds with seldom fewer than twenty members. Several female breeding herds may join to form loosely knit clans; male-based bachelor herds split temporarily during the breeding season.

Opposite: *The southern carmine bee-eater is a highly gregarious, intra-African migrant which comes to the Delta in spring to breed, the Panhandle being one of its prime breeding sites. The nest of this brilliantly coloured little bird is situated at the end of a burrow, which it excavates in a cliff-like sandbank to a depth of up to 4 metres. Some breeding colonies contain more than a thousand birds, and the considerable noise they generate attracts numerous predators. The greatest threat to the nests comes from monitor lizards, which eat both eggs and chicks: these large reptiles pay little heed to the bee-eaters' tactic of mass-mobbing potential predators, and are probably accountable for a large proportion of the chick mortality in the region.*

Above: *Another gregarious species, the masked weaver, assembles in large breeding colonies, particularly when nesting over water. Males have up to four mates per season and, during the breeding season, constantly try to lure potential mates to the nests they have built.*

A sub-adult member of the Dead Tree lion pride, whose territory is centred on Xakanaxa, nuzzles his sibling after returning from a brief tree-climbing expedition. It is thought that the complex social relationships within mammalian society are maintained in part through mutual grooming and other forms of physical contact. Members of lion prides often split into temporary sub-groups and whenever members meet or are reunited – even after sleeping apart for a few hours – a ceremony of rubbing and licking, accompanied by vocal huffing and moaning, takes place. This physical contact is usually initiated by lower-ranking pride members.

Almost identical social and breeding systems exist within wild dog and dwarf mongoose populations. Both species form packs of related individuals supplemented by immigrants. Unusually for social carnivores, breeding within each pack is almost totally monopolised by a dominant pair, and subordinate animals instead help to rear this pair's offspring. It is more profitable for subordinate animals to help a dominant, close relative to breed successfully than to try to start a new pack and breed

themselves. By providing food for the young animals and standing guard at den sites, the non-breeding pack members also enable the lactating alpha female to forage for herself and better meet her considerable energy requirements. Dwarf mongoose females have even higher energy requirements as they often fall pregnant while still lactating. To compensate for this, subordinate dwarf mongoose females occasionally lactate and provide milk for another's young, even when they have not yet produced their own litters.

Social interactions between elephants involve a lot of physical contact. Each evening elephant bulls emerge from the woodlands and gather at the drying end of the Khwai River to drink. Before quenching their thirst the bulls go through an elaborate greeting ceremony, with each animal inserting the tip of its trunk into the mouths of other elephant.

Although waterbuck rams are territorial, they sometimes tolerate the presence of several bachelor males within their territories and, occasionally, even within their female herds. The condition of this tolerance is that the non-territorial males are totally submissive, an attitude usually demonstrated by a show of appeasement. The territorial ram, on the left, holds his head high and glowers down at the submissive ram. Failure to perform this ceremony will undoubtedly result in a territorial clash.

Touch is an important aspect of interaction between social animals, helping both to develop bonds and to establish and maintain hierarchies between individuals. Individuals of all ages within impala herds, for example, frequently indulge in bouts of mutual grooming, and pairs of impala take turns grooming each other's neck and face.

Although mutual grooming is to a large extent symbolic, animals also need to groom themselves in order to rid their bodies of parasites and to heal wounds. Birds, furthermore, need to maintain the condition of their feathers, and aquatic birds preen themselves to keep their feathers waterproof. To dry off after bathing, many birds will stand at the water's edge with their wings outstretched, as this spur-winged goose (above) is doing. In some cases a mutually beneficial grooming relationship develops between members of different species, whereby one animal depends on another to keep itself free of parasites, and the latter animal relies on having access to the parasites for food. The grooming of this giraffe here by yellow-billed and red-billed oxpeckers (right) is a typical example of such behaviour.

TERRITORIALITY

In a rare show of aggression, a tiny malachite kingfisher issues a threat display for the benefit of another intruding kingfisher. Territories are vigorously defended against other individuals of the same species to ensure that the holders of the territory have sole access to the breeding and feeding opportunities within that area. The bird depicted here regularly hunted small fish from this perch overhanging the Okavango River, downstream from Shakawe.

Opposite: *Hippo tend to express territorial aggression in a wide range of ritualised displays, and submissive individuals usually give way before serious physical combat is called for. Here, in a less serious sparring session between adolescent males, two hippos test each other's strength for future reference.*

Above, below and overleaf: *In the breeding season, between January and March, red lechwe rams stake out temporary territories. Here, two males near Fourth Bridge engage in a fierce territorial dispute. Sparring sessions are prolonged and rage over land and water, and the eventual loser is evicted from the territory.*

Above: *In the middle of the dry season, fish trapped in the last dwindling pools of the Khwai River attract hordes of waterbirds. The pair of saddle-billed storks featured in these three pictures rapidly established a tentative territory centred on a profitable pool and defended its waters and fish supply from all other birds. A particularly persistent grey heron, though, regularly returned to the pool after being chased over the surrounding camelthorn woodlands by one of the storks.*

Below: *Unable to defend the vast home ranges they occupy, chacma baboons are not considered territorial. Social interactions within a baboon troop, however, are among the most complex in the animal kingdom. The various relationships develop constantly and define hierarchies within the troop. Male baboons, up to double the size of females, all hold higher rank than females. The latter form alliances with troop males – subtle relationships established and maintained through grooming – that pay dividends when the solicited male comes to the aid of the female and her offspring whenever competition occurs within the troop.*

Two Burchell's zebra stallions engage in a dominance struggle, south of Third Bridge. A herd stallion usually presides over a harem, comprising up to six mares and their foals. Although zebra are not overly territorial, fights do sometimes break out between stallions when a rival tries to abduct one of the harem mares. The contests are protracted affairs involving rearing up on their hind legs, wrestling and biting, and continue until the weaker stallion capitulates – usually through injury or exhaustion. Harem mares, however, generally associate for life, and the herd structure changes only if the presiding stallion is displaced.

A small pool in the northern Panhandle, formerly used by the Mohembo villagers as a mokoro *station, forms a lucrative fishing spot for egrets. A strict hierarchy orders the members of this exclusive avian fishing community, with slaty egrets dominant. Fierce struggles ensue whenever new birds arrive at the pool, as this contest between two black egrets demonstrates.*

Right: *In areas where they occur in high densities, such as the Okavango, male tsessebe are highly territorial. These antelope use a range of methods to demonstrate territorial tenure. The most commonly seen involves a male standing statue-like on a termite mound. Here, a male looks up from scraping its horns on the ground, another form of territorial advertisement and one which is particularly favoured when the ground is muddy.*

Below: *At the edge of the old airstrip at Xakanaxa, a lioness of the Dead Tree pride roars at the cold dawn. The roar of a lion, heard from near or far, is the Okavango's most stirring sound. The roar serves a range of purposes, including intimidating rivals and helping pride members to contact each other; but its most obvious role lies in advertising territorial tenure.*

COURTSHIP AND BREEDING

A gomoti or water fig island in the middle of Xakanaxa lagoon provides an ideal roosting and nesting spot for a bewildering array of egrets, herons and storks. Most waterbirds within the Delta time their breeding to coincide with the dissipation of the annual floodwaters, when fish trapped in the region's dwindling pools provide ample sustenance for the growing chicks.

Left: *The breeding habits of the African jacana are among the more unusual in the bird world. The bird is a polyandrous species, meaning that a single female can have more than one partner; sometimes a jacana will have up to six partners at any given time. During the breeding season noisy chases involving jacanas are seen over most open waters in the Delta, as males stake out territories and eject competing birds. Once a female has been attracted to a territory, pairs mate up to seven times a day (middle). The males incubate clutches of up to four scribble-covered caramel eggs on a nest constructed on floating vegetation (bottom). Although the eggs have a special pore structure that prevents them from becoming waterlogged, the male folds his wings under the eggs while incubating to protect them from the wet nest floor. The responsibility of raising the chicks falls entirely on the male jacana. The burden is lessened significantly, though, as the precocial chicks are basically independent a few hours after birth and rely on the male for protection only. During the first few weeks of their lives, the chicks will be gathered under the male's wings if danger threatens.*

The female baboon's menstrual cycle lasts 36 days, and while she is in oestrus her genital area becomes red and swollen. Although she is generally receptive to all males and may mate up to 100 times during each oestrus period, the individuals most likely to consort with her at this time are dominant males and those males with whom she has established alliances (above). After a gestation period of about five months, a single, black-haired infant is born. A young baboon is nursed for about six months and is initially carried between its mother's legs; later it begins to ride, jockey-style, on her back (below), only starting to move and play more independently at the age of three or four months.

Left: *As the breeding season approaches, impala bachelor herds break up and rams stake out territories containing resources that should entice female herds. During May the dryland areas of the Okavango resound with the roaring and grunting of impala rams in rut. These extraordinary sounds accompany the numerous fights and chases that erupt as the rams defend their territories. In the Okavango, impala rutting is confined to a short period immediately preceding and following the mating peak, after which their overt territoriality diminishes and bachelor herds re-form.*

Opposite: *At sunset on one of the countless water fig tree islands that dot the lagoons of the Okavango, a little egret displays its delicate 'aigrettes'. Such changes in plumage serve primarily to make the male more attractive during the breeding season. These filament-like white plumes, which decorate the bird's back, were in great demand during the nineteenth century when they were used to decorate hats.*

Overleaf: *In a seasonal channel near Xakanaxa, two crocodiles perform their elegant, slowly unfolding courtship ritual. By raising her head high out of the water, the female is making a typically submissive crocodile gesture which, when accompanied by a drawn-out growl, is indicative of her acceptance of the courting male.*

Sub-adult male lions commonly form coalitions on leaving their natal pride to strengthen their chances of procuring a pride when mature. Pride tenure is normally as brief as two years, before the dominant males are in turn deposed. The new dominant males will often kill all cubs within a pride so that the offspring in the pride are guaranteed to be their own, and so that they can begin producing offspring themselves as soon as possible. If they lose their cubs, lionesses come into heat soon afterwards, but will not conceive until the males have proved themselves capable of successfully defending their new pride and territory. There is no hierarchical access to breeding rights amongst coalition members, and the first male to meet an oestrous female usually becomes her consort. A lioness typically mates with her consort up to three times an hour for the duration of her five-day oestrus period. Here, a Dead Tree pride lioness seduces one of the pride's pair of magnificent black-maned males at the onset of courtship (left). At times during courtship, the massive males are rendered meek and mild as lionesses are prone to bouts of aggression and frequently lash out when they tire of the males' constant attention (above).

Opposite: *Giraffe herds are loosely knit societies with constantly changing membership, and consequently, courtship and mating are among the infrequent occasions on which adult giraffes associate closely. Hormone levels in a female's urine serve as a gauge of her reproductive status, and dominant males, who usually have exclusive access to breeding privileges, constantly examine each cow's disposition to mating. When a bull finds a female in oestrus he becomes her constant companion – the pair shown here stayed together for three days before the bull attempted to mount the female. A single calf is born after a gestation period of about fifteen months.*

Right: *A forest of drowned trees in Santawani forms the backdrop to the graceful mating dance of an ostrich pair. Ostrich hens normally lay their eggs in a communal nest which is incubated in turn by the members of a dominant pair. The hen incubating the nest recognises her own eggs and manoeuvres them to the centre of the clutch, thereby ensuring that her own eggs are less likely to fall victim to predation.*

Above: *A pair of African fish eagles mate near their nest in a knobthorn overlooking the Khwai River. Fish eagle pairs use the same nest each breeding season; in one notable case a nest was used for over thirty years.*

Left: *A shallow nest scrape near Mohembo reveals a clutch of African skimmer eggs. Apart from falling victim to voracious natural predators like fish eagles and monitor lizards, skimmer nests also come under threat from human disturbance, and these birds have lost suitable nesting sites throughout their traditional southern African breeding range. The Okavango River and some smaller pans within the Delta are now their safest breeding haven, but even here their nesting methods render them vulnerable. Local children have been observed using live chicks as fishing bait, but a recently launched education programme intends to discourage this gruesome and thoughtless behaviour.*

Opposite: *Bearing a freshly caught grub, a male hoopoe returns to its nest within a hollow tree branch to feed its newly hatched chicks. Female hoopoes rarely leave their nest until their chicks are at least quarter-grown.*

Above: *Though little studied, side-striped jackal appear to have fascinating social and breeding systems. They exhibit highly territorial behaviour, and breeding pairs probably mate for life. Pup mortality is thought to be high, but some surviving pups remain in their natal territory, helping their parents to rear the next litter by bringing food – either whole or regurgitated – back to weaned pups in the den. To reduce predation, dens are moved frequently; the jackals shown here changed dens twice in three weeks.*

Right: *After a seven-month gestation period, lechwe calves are born on dry land and, apart from morning and evening suckling sessions, remain hidden for about three weeks. Only then do they join the herd, forming crèches quite independent from their mothers.*

Above: *Because of the vervet monkey's relatively long gestation period – almost five months – the young are noticeably precocious and more advanced than other monkeys at birth. Here, a baby vervet with distinctive dark hair suckles from its mother in the rain.*

Chacma baboons

PLAY

Play is the facet of animal behaviour that humans can relate to most easily, and it is also one of the easiest to identify. Although at first glance play seems to serve little practical purpose, biologists assume that it stimulates physical and mental growth. Even so, it is almost impossible to state this with certainty as these developments are manifest only much later in life. However, a lot of energy is expended in this pursuit, and considerable risks are involved – including sustaining injury during high-spirited play and attracting unwanted attention from predators, against which the players are normally too young to be able to defend themselves. For these two reasons alone we can deduce that this activity must clearly benefit the animals at some stage.

Play seems to occur most often among the more sociable and intelligent animals. Thus, there is a higher incidence among mammals than among other creatures, although a few bird species have also been observed indulging in play. As it is usually youngsters that are involved, this activity is thought to be a significant learning tool. It could also be that, with food and protection being provided by their parents, younger animals simply have more time and energy at their disposal. One can also broaden the definition of play to include the investigation of new and unfamiliar surroundings, prompted by curiosity.

Play in animals can be conceptualised in terms of three basic categories: object play, social play and chase play.

Usually the first type of play in which any young animal involves itself is object play. As soon as its senses have developed sufficiently and it emerges from the protection of its mother, a young animal is confronted with a wealth of interesting objects: everything it encounters, from a piece of grass to an animal of another species, is potentially novel to its experience. Interaction with its immediate surroundings takes the form of investigation and is thought to help the animal to categorise things and experiences in terms of usefulness and risk.

Object play has the potential to develop into social play. When an animal finds something or takes possession of an object during play it almost always tries to entice its siblings with it, the aim being to interest them enough that they try to appropriate the object. If an object fails to elicit this response from siblings it is often abandoned in favour of something more interesting. Wrestling frequently develops around these play objects and probably teaches those involved other crucial skills. In carnivores, for instance, wrestling with objects is thought to develop the hunting skills that are so important for adults. Social play also seems to help establish a social hierarchy – as the animals grow older, wrestling and play-fighting develop and patterns of dominance by certain individuals emerge. Play-fighting in this context is thought to reduce the need to establish dominance by fighting in earnest at a later stage in life, when the fights can be more severe and the risk of serious injury much greater.

The most dynamic form of play, and the one most likely to involve older members of the young animals' social circle, is chase play. Repeated over and over again, chase play helps to develop a young animal's strength, co-ordination and athletic abilities, as well as familiarising the youngster with its habitat. It also builds resourcefulness and inventiveness in response to rapidly changing circumstances. Both carnivores and herbivores practise chase play, to develop responses as hunter and hunted respectively. Animals of other species are often – but rarely willingly – involved in chase play. When this happens, play informs the instigator of the chase about the reactions of other species and establishes early on the status quo of inter-species relationships.

Another common feature of play behaviour in animals is that it is undertaken only by healthy individuals; furthermore, the presence or absence of play in animal populations is thought to be an indicator of the health of their immediate environment.

Notwithstanding the various theories concerning this behaviour, there remains the possibility that play could simply be indulged in for the fun of it!

Impala

Previous pages: *One of a pair of juvenile black-backed jackals, playing near their den in Santawani, nips its sibling. Such gestures of low-key aggression can be seen as a precedent for hunting behaviour in adults.*

Opposite: *A gang of juvenile baboons chase each other up and around a raintree. Not above 'playing dirty', the youngster hanging from the* broken-off branch on the right reaches down to kick a smaller playmate in the face as it tries to climb the tree.*

Above: *Two juvenile lions engage in an early morning sparring session at Xakanaxa. Such playful wrestling and sparring helps to establish a hierarchy of sorts that will persist later in life.*

Previous pages: *To reduce mortality rates amongst their young, impala females drop their lambs within days of each other. Against a lush green backdrop, crèches of newborn lambs participate in mass chases, practising the athletic skills they will need to evade predators. Adults often join in these exuberant relays across the floodplains.*

Opposite: *Still acquiring its parents' arboreal agility, a young vervet monkey gets stuck between two trees.*

Right: *Objects chosen for play seem to be those that elicit the most interest from other youngsters. This young spotted hyaena tried and abandoned several twigs before its elder sibling was enticed into joining the game.*

Below: *A wild dog yearling tests the interest value of a branch.*

Overleaf: *Elephant relish any encounter with water or mud, and their enjoyment when drinking, bathing or wallowing is palpable.*

Hamerkop

Red lechwe

Egyptian geese

Red lechwe

MIGRATIONS AND MOVEMENTS

Migration is the regular seasonal movement of animals from one place to another, and is undertaken for two main reasons: so that localised and transient food sources can be exploited most effectively, and so that suitable breeding grounds can be found.

As the cycle of wet and dry seasons progresses, the food and water resources in any given area change. Driven by instinct and memory, animals move – often in massed herds – to where conditions are best: to areas of recent rainfall, where they can feast on new grazing and fresh water, and in the dry season, to areas with a permanent water supply. As well as providing the animals with better resources, these movements relieve pressure on the grazing lands, enabling them to recover, when the animals move on, in time for their return.

In the harsh Kalahari landscape that surrounds the Okavango, migration is common among animals that are not specifically adapted to life in arid conditions. In the past, zebra, wildebeest, buffalo and elephant undertook significant seasonal movements, but most of these have been severely curtailed in the last few decades by the erection of veterinary cordon fences across their time-honoured migration routes. At times the movements have taken on life-and-death significance when drought conditions or fires have driven the animals from their range. Tragically, the animals of the Kalahari can no longer escape the conflagrations – in 1996 thousands of animals died along the northern boundary fence of the Central Kalahari Game Reserve, trying to escape a fire that ravaged the area. Much publicised wildebeest die-offs along the same fence have occurred several times when the animals, trying to escape drought conditions in the reserve, failed in their attempt to reach permanent water to the north.

However, regular seasonal movements still take place within the Okavango system. The Delta undergoes a unique seasonal metamorphosis which provides its animal inhabitants with a supply of good resources all year round. The herbivores of the Okavango cover substantial distances within the area, according to the time of year and the progress of the annual flood. The wet season sees the animals disperse into the woodlands, where sweet grazing and fresh water are plentiful, but as the dry season approaches they are forced to move back to the edge of the permanent Delta. This margin fluctuates considerably with the inundation from Angola, and soon after the waters have receded, large expanses of fresh grazing appear. The herbivores drawn here by the new growth in turn attract predators, which follow the herds as they move.

Again though, a man-made barrier seems set to alter this natural movement: the new Northern Buffalo Fence, which skirts the northern edge of the Delta, has recently been closed, effectively ending the traditional movements of buffalo and elephant to and from wet season havens in Namibia's Caprivi Strip.

The birds of the Okavango, however, are not confined by fences, and extensive migrations still take place. Attracted by ideal conditions in the summer months, most of the migrants arrive from far afield, though a handful of species travel much shorter distances. Some migrations occur so that the birds can avail themselves of better food or water resources, while others are in response to breeding conditions, or to a combination of these factors – breeding migrants time their arrival to coincide with the abundance of food available towards the end of the dry season. Ideal weather conditions, especially good rainfall, stimulate breeding on a large scale, particularly among waterbirds; conversely drought can inhibit breeding in many bird species. Of the numerous species that come to the Okavango to breed, the carmine bee-eaters, African skimmers and woodland kingfishers are probably the most evident, and the distinctive, high-pitched, bubbling call and wing displays produced by the woodland kingfisher as the bird desperately seeks a mate herald the start of the Okavango spring. The yellow-billed stork, a commonly seen species in these parts, has its primary southern African breeding ground in the Delta.

Most migrant birds arrive in the Delta towards the end of winter, when the resources of the surrounding lands are starting to run dry, and stay during the summer months, when they can take advantage of the food and water that still exist in abundance here. The spreading flood lures birds to the floodplains as fish head into these shallow areas to breed. Later, as the floodplains dry up, young fish become exposed and birds once again move into these areas to feed. Similarly, waterholes provide the focus of activity during winter as birds congregate to catch the fish trapped in the dwindling pools. Pelicans and storks are particularly active in these movements and will fly far to seek out better seasonal food supplies.

Chacma baboon

Of course, movements on a smaller scale take place on a daily basis, as animals move between their feeding grounds and their resting places. Notable examples are the hippo and the elephant, which make regular trails through the swamps and contribute to channel formation. Baboons roost in the cover of the forest canopy at night then roam widely by day, and numerous bird species undertake similar local movements.

Impala

Movement is one of the constants within the Okavango system. In response to the ever-changing landscape, the region's inhabitants gather in numbers, fly vast distances, ford floodplains and channels, and rumble through forests. The whistling of a thousand pairs of quelea wings, the thunder of an elephant herd charging over a floodplain and the quiet ripple of a lion pride swimming across a channel all bear testament to their supreme adaptability.

Spotted hyaena

Above: *Disturbed by some unseen incident, an elephant herd thunders over a flooded* molapo. *Charging elephants can reach speeds of up to 40 kilometres per hour, but a herd normally adjusts its speed to match that of its slowest members.*

Left: *While running, warthog hold their tufted tails erect. Unless they are under threat, these animals prefer to trot well below their reputed top speed of 60 kilometres per hour.*

Above and below: *The abundance of water throughout the Okavango requires its inhabitants to cross inundated floodplains and channels regularly. A young lion near Nxabega, on the edge of the seasonal Delta, pauses before swimming across a channel to rejoin his pride, which had chased a herd of buffalo across the water the previous evening. The threat of being attacked by crocodile while swimming is very real, and although lion regularly swim in the Delta environment, they never do so without first scanning the water carefully.*

Left: *The unfolding elegance of a cattle egret launching into flight is frozen by the camera motordrive. Wherever slow-moving herds of large herbivores are found, flocks of cattle egrets occur in abundance. In fact, this is one wildlife species which has benefitted from the modern expansion of commercial cattle operations, and populations of this bird have spread worldwide. Cattle egrets forage around the herbivores' hooves, hawking the insects the cattle disturb while feeding. Occasionally, the birds temporarily suspend foraging and flock to a nearby tree to preen.*

Overleaf: *Pink-backed pelicans swoop down to begin foraging from a shrinking pool.*

Left and below: *Throughout the Delta, red-billed queleas gather in massed flocks of tens of thousands. Often mistaken for columns of smoke from veld fires, the seed-eating flocks forage in boisterous waves over the Delta's grasslands. At night they roost in thorn trees and come under assault from virtually all carnivores. By day, predators collect the carcasses of hundreds of birds killed by the flock's crush, the victims often found grotesquely impaled on the thorns of the trees in which they roost. The flocks shown here are viewed from the ground along the Gomoti River and from the air near Betsha.*

As their name suggests, waterbuck are commonly found where water is abundant, as it is in the Okavango. Their second essential habitat requirement – high quality grazing – is in relatively short supply here, though, and this probably accounts for the species' low profile in the region. Waterbuck do not move at any great pace, relying instead on cover to elude predators. Here, a female waterbuck follows her herd across a narrow channel.

Recent immigrants to a Fourth Bridge floodplain, a herd of Burchell's zebra rushes to a nearby rainwater pool to drink. Within the Okavango ecosystem, zebra regularly undertake seasonal migrations, attracted to areas of recent rainfall by the fresh grazing available. While moving, the dominant mare leads a single-file procession arranged according to rank, while the herd stallion brings up the rear.

During the dry season, the Khwai River is the lifeline of the eastern extremities of the Okavango – a thin finger of the Delta running through otherwise dry woodlands. Each morning and evening small herds of sable antelope emerge from the surrounding woodlands to drink.

Further south, in the remote drylands near the boundary of Moremi Game Reserve, a herd of wildebeest unused to the presence of vehicles flees across a desiccated floodplain.

Above: *Although hippo spend much of the day wallowing in water or mud, at night they move away from their aquatic refuges to forage on land. Treading well-worn paths to regular feeding grounds, they can cover up to 10 kilometres a night, although an average feeding trip does not go as far afield. These bulky creatures appear ungainly on land but can, under threat, reach speeds approaching 30 kilometres per hour.*

Right: *The classic Okavango image: a red lechwe ram flees across a shallow flood-plain. Specially adapted hooves and strong hindquarters allow lechwe to run faster through water than on land, and they readily enter water in an attempt to escape pursuing predators.*

Opposite: *Carmine bee-eaters are regular breeding migrants in the Okavango, and these brilliantly coloured birds provide a spectacular sight when they come here to nest* en masse. *Here, a flock of carmine bee-eaters takes flight from a flat-ground nesting site near Xakanaxa lagoon. Although predators like monitor lizards regularly plunder the nests, the bee-eaters readily mob large animals like elephants, forcing them to circumnavigate their nesting site.*

Right: *Aspects of flight: a little egret returns to roost in a water fig thicket; a hooded vulture vacates its perch in a tree and descends towards an elephant carcass; and a three-banded plover takes off from the edge of a rainwater pan.*

Lioness

THE QUEST FOR SUSTENANCE

The search for food and water is a constant preoccupation of the many creatures that inhabit the Okavango. Animals all have their own areas of specialisation, and no two species can co-exist using exactly the same resources, in the same way, at the same time. The three main feeding categories among animals – carnivores, herbivores and omnivores – are well known, and as animals specialise, further subdivisions emerge: carnivores fall into the basic categories of hunters and scavengers, and herbivores are browsers and grazers, though in many species there is a degree of overlap. The form and food preferences of every animal go hand in hand: size and shape, digestive, social and reproductive systems, feeding choices and techniques differ from species to species, and each of these factors enables an animal to exploit its chosen ecological niche most efficiently. Specialisation in turn places particular demands on an animal, which it must adapt to in order to survive. Those that subsist on plant matter have had to develop enhanced vigilance in order to stand the best possible chance against the carnivores. The latter have in turn had to acquire various effective hunting techniques: some hunt at night, some maximise their efficiency by hunting in packs and others have developed tremendous speed.

Elephant

Some species spend more time engaged in the search for food than others. Most antelope, for instance, spend more than two-thirds of the day feeding and digesting food. Lion, on the other hand, hunt only occasionally, and because they derive their nutrition in a far more concentrated form from prey than herbivores do from plant matter, they spend most of their time sleeping. Even within genera there is a marked differentiation of feeding techniques. Some kinds of heron move about frantically catching masses of small fish, while the goliath heron catches just two or three larger fish, and will even ignore smaller ones that swim within its range. Each behaviour is an adaptation evolved to exploit the available resources in a unique way.

Helmeted guineafowl

Life in the Okavango demands other adaptations from its inhabitants. In response to the shifting distribution of herbivores in the Delta, predators like lion, hyaena and leopard all cross water frequently to follow their prey; apart from showing a slight wariness of crocodiles they enter the water readily, even though cats in other environments are well known to have a natural aversion to getting wet.

As in any ecosystem, the creatures that live in the Okavango are those best able to take advantage of the resources available here. The abundance of fish in the Delta attracts a range of waterbirds that specialise in eating fish. Raptors such as fish eagles and Pel's fishing owls exploit this food source too, hunting at different times of the day to maximise the resource. Pygmy geese occur at a higher density in the Okavango than anywhere else because their preferred food, the seed of the waterlily, is in plentiful supply here.

In the Okavango Delta, access to drinking water, the other important part of an animal's nutrient requirements, is seldom a problem. The continually shifting patterns of water distribution within the system, though, demand that game constantly move to different areas. As well as seasonal changes in water distribution, significant long-term shifts also occur. A lodge in the Santawani area, south of Moremi Game Reserve, for example, used to offer *mokoro* trips, but today the forlorn jetty stands in a dry channel and the nearest permanent water is 20 kilometres away. Nevertheless, the wildlife is still prolific here, though its composition has changed and the animals that remain have adapted their habits to take into account the lack of a ready water supply.

White-backed vultures

Previous pages: *In a startling demonstration of hunting adaptations, a black egret extends its wings to form a canopy, under which it searches for fish. The canopy is thought to lure fish into the deceptive safety of its shade, where they are easily picked off; the fish is also possibly attracted by the bird wiggling its bright, yellow toes.*

Opposite: *An elephant bull in the Khwai area systematically strips the bark off an umbrella thorn. He effortlessly prises each piece of bark free with a tusk before peeling it back to the tree crown until the entire tree is ringbarked – a feeding technique that will eventually result in the tree's death. Recent research has indicated, however, that bark does not account for a high percentage of an elephant's dietary intake.*

Right: *Near Nxabega, an area well endowed with* Hyphaene *palms, an elephant bull shakes a palm stem to dislodge the fruit that grows beneath its fronds. A delicacy much favoured by elephant, the fruit, locally known as vegetable ivory, can take up to four years to mature and fall from the tree. Elephant are important agents in the dispersal and germination of these and other seeds, as the seeds seem to germinate more successfully having passed through an elephant's digestive tract.*

Overleaf: *An African fish eagle plucks a barbel from the edge of Qhaaxhwa lagoon. The eagle swoops down from a perch over the water to take fish swimming close to the surface, then carries its prey back to its perch to devour it at leisure. If the fish is too heavy to carry, rather than abandoning the catch the eagle will swim through the water and drag it to the shore.*

Above: *Surrounded by jacanas and ducks, a group of lechwe nibble on aquatic vegetation growing on the edge of Mmaleswana Pan. As well as feeding in water that sometimes reaches up to their bellies, lechwe graze on the flush of new grasses that grow in the wake of the receding flood.*

Left: *Steenbok are not as dependent on water as other antelope are, and consequently are normally found in the Delta's drier regions, either browsing or grazing. Although these antelope are usually found in pairs, this lone animal is content to reach for a tasty morsel from a thorn tree without company.*

Above: *Acacias are the dietary mainstays of giraffe. In this case, a giraffe stoops to grasp the deciduous leaves from a candlepod acacia. Giraffes' long necks enable them to browse an exclusive band of foliage beyond the reach of all other herbivores except elephant, while its 45-centimetre-long prehensile tongue extends its reach even further.*

Right: *A green pigeon, seldom seen because of its habit of feeding in dense tree crowns, is lured into view by the fruit of a common wild fig, its favourite food. The bird is thought to undertake significant local migrations to find fig trees in fruit.*

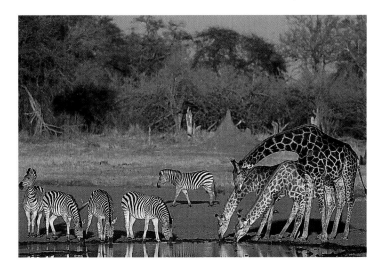

Above: *As the evening light fades, a mixed herd of zebra and giraffe gathers to drink from the Khwai River. Although a giraffe's height places it at a distinct advantage while feeding, it leaves the animal particularly vulnerable while drinking. Giraffe consequently approach water with caution, and painstakingly scan the entire area before daring to splay their legs and drink. Owing to the high moisture content of their selected browse, however, they are not as dependent on water as zebra are.*

Left: *Another of the Delta's drying pools attracted these white pelicans and spoonbills foraging abreast. For two days the pool was a writhing mass of activity as flocks arrived to feast on its trapped fish. Then, suddenly, the birds moved on to more productive feeding grounds, leaving the pool deserted. The spoonbill moves erratically along the water's edge, sweeping its open bill from side to side across the water and snapping closed on any edible objects it encounters. White pelican flocks, conversely, spread out across a pool and systematically drive fish into the shallows where they can easily be picked off.*

Above and left: *Dense populations of immature raptors, such as the tawny eagle* (left) *and bateleur* (above), *inexplicably frequent the eastern end of the Khwai River. During the hottest part of the day raptors ordinarily gather around water to drink and bathe; along the edge of Khwai River though, it is not uncommon to find gatherings of fifteen bateleurs or more. Part of this particular stretch of water's attraction may be the large flocks of doves that also collect there to drink. The raptors constantly attack the preoccupied flocks and almost inevitably succeed.*

Below: *Still not fully awake after leaving their nocturnal roosts, two young baboons stoop to quench their thirst together.*

Above and overleaf: *Lions derive most of their moisture requirements
from their prey's body fluids, but if they encounter water they will not
hesitate to drink. For cats though, drinking is a drawn-out process; they
can only take in small volumes of liquid with each lap, as their rough
tongues are not well adapted to the task.*

Right: *A waterbuck ram pauses to drink from a narrow channel.
Although they are not as aquatic as lechwe and sitatunga, waterbuck
have unusually high water requirements and are seldom found far
from a source.*

Opposite: *Rather unusually for its species, a male Bennett's woodpecker examines a tree trunk for potential food. This woodpecker usually forages on the ground, feeding almost exclusively on ants and termites. When it does forage on branches and trunks it takes prey from the wood surface, unlike other woodpeckers which excavate insects and larvae from beneath bark with their bills or extricate them with long, sticky tongues. Although these woodpeckers occur widely throughout the region, they are thinly spread as each family group maintains a large territory.*

Right: *An African wild dog feeds on the remains of the second impala lamb its pack killed within 15 minutes. Impala account for up to 85 percent of the prey of this fascinating and superbly efficient hunter in the Okavango. Each hunt begins with a ritualised pack greeting and a search for prey, with the final chase beginning only when the selected prey takes flight. Experienced dogs normally will abandon a chase within a kilometre if the quarry has not yet been caught. Compared with most other predators, wild dogs have a fairly organised system when it comes to behaviour around a kill, with younger dogs being allowed to feed first.*

Above and left: *Unlike the smaller vervet monkey, baboons are very capable hunters, often taking small mammals such as newborn antelope. However, they are primarily vegetarian and take advantage of any local food abundance. In these two images from the Xakanaxa region, a young male retrieves succulent grass roots from a pan recently inundated by the annual flood, and a baboon relishes an enormous mushroom expertly removed from within a termite mound.*

Although vervet monkeys are omnivorous, their diet is largely vegetarian – forays into meat-eating are usually restricted to insects and small vertebrates like lizards and bird nestlings. This male vervet, however, was found feeding on a tree squirrel and refused to relinquish it, even when a passing leopard disturbed the foraging troop.

Left: *A young leopard pauses over the massive lechwe ram its mother has recently killed. Leopard usually move their kills into trees to protect them from other predators, but this carcass proved too big for either cat to move. Despite standing guard over their kill for the entire day and covering it with sand in a bid to hide it from intrusive vultures, by the next morning all that remained at the kill site was a confusion of hyaena spoor.*

Above: *In the prelude to a stalk, in this case to ambush a sibling, a young lion inexpertly adopts the low profile required for hunting. Lions undergo a complete metamorphosis when they are intent on killing, making it difficult to reconcile the lazy, prone forms of the sleeping cats with the awesome power exuded by hunting lions.*

Anatomy of a kill. Above left: *A male lion eagerly follows the progress of an unfolding chase.* Above right, below and overleaf: *I left these lions sleeping under a raintree in Santawani, but by the time I returned less than twenty minutes later, they had killed and almost completely devoured a female waterbuck, which had probably stumbled on the pride while they slept. Lion are the ultimate opportunists, taking prey whenever it is available, even if they have recently fed. The scene around* a fresh kill is seldom a tranquil affair, as pride bonds are forgotten and each lion fights for its place around the carcass. Often individuals will remove pieces of the carcass to consume away from the mêlée. If the kill is too small for the entire pride to feed on, weaker lions lose out: lionesses do not even relinquish places to their own cubs. In the aftermath of the kill, though, pride bonds are reinforced with obvious displays of affection and mutual grooming.

Above: *One would think that this elephant carcass, not far from the Khwai River, would be a windfall for the seven spotted hyaena cubs waiting at a nearby den, but although spotted hyaenas sometimes take pickings from a carcass back to their dens, these are seldom for the cubs' benefit. Instead, the young rely on their mother's milk, which provides more energy than the milk of any other land mammal, until they are over a year old.*

Right: *An impressive lappet-faced vulture arrives and immediately imposes its authority at the carcass. Looming giants compared to other vultures, and always the dominant bird at a carcass, lappet-faced vultures often arrive later than the other vultures. Their strong bills are well adapted to feeding on the skin and bones that normally remain though.*

Epilogue

Okavango
under threat

In the comfort of one of the many lodges that dot the mainland, floodplains and islands of the Okavango Delta, it is all too easy to take the continued existence of this vast wetland wilderness for granted. Inevitably though, one's thoughts turn to the countless threats that face this magnificent place. Discounting them is easy. All too often these days we read in the media about environmental degradation and developments in the human arena that threaten the world's last remaining natural areas. Unfortunately these issues are often considered relatively minor alongside other lead stories, but the dangers discussed are nevertheless all too real. The Okavango is no stranger to them, and it seems miraculous that the region has survived so many challenges. Its continued survival, however, is by no means guaranteed, as it is largely through what one observer has termed 'benign neglect' that the Delta has emerged in the latter part of the twentieth century as one of the last remaining pristine wilderness areas in the world.

Since their introduction into the country, long before its borders were demarcated, cattle have dominated the culture and economy of Botswana, and the country's cattle industry approaches the new millennium in a very healthy state. Today, the destinies of the cattle industry and the Okavango are intimately entwined.

Herdsmen and their cattle have traditionally led relatively nomadic lives, dictated largely by the availability of accessible grazing and water. Initially this restricted herd sizes naturally, but improvements in the water supply, brought about by the sinking of numerous boreholes in the Kalahari rangelands, opened up extensive new grazing areas, allowing large numbers of cattle to congregate on previously barren land and degrade the surrounding habitat through overgrazing. As a direct result of range expansion, and despite the opinion expressed by many critics that the Kalahari environment is poorly suited to commercial cattle-farming operations, the size of the national herd has exploded.

The commercialisation and expansion of the cattle industry in Botswana began when the country was a British Protectorate, and gained momentum after it became a major beneficiary of the 1975 Lomé agreements with the European Union (EU). The agreements have effectively resulted in the EU paying preferential rates of up to 60 percent more than the going world rate for Botswanan beef, through a range of subsidies and tariff refunds, and providing substantial financial assistance for stock purchases, borehole development and land-leasing. These subsidies have been instrumental in establishing and entrenching the cattle industry, and the national herd now numbers more than 3 000 000 animals. Despite claims that only a few large cattle barons – and not the farming community at large – benefit from them, the subsidies continue. One enigma that remains in this situation is why the EU is providing these considerable subsidies and incentives when it has a substantial beef surplus of its own.

Undoubtedly the most negative consequence of the agreements has been the long threads of veterinary cordon fences that now criss-cross the country. The terms of the agreements require that Botswana adhere to European disease-control initiatives, designed in the most part to prevent the infection of cattle with foot-and-mouth disease. Consequently, wildlife (thought to be vectors of the disease) and cattle have to be kept apart. This has been achieved by the erection of several thousand kilometres of fencing across the country, much of which bisects traditional wildlife migration routes though the wilderness.

It is common knowledge that large numbers of antelope have died at some of the fences while seeking water during droughts, the most notable die-off being of the wildebeest of the Central Kalahari Game Reserve. In a somewhat belated attempt to prevent further such die-offs, the Department of Wildlife & National Parks (DWNP) has established a number of boreholes in the national parks most affected, in the hope that year-round access to water will make the region's wildlife more sedentary. In a notable turning of the tables, during similar drought periods in the Okavango region in the early 1980s the fences in fact ensured that cattle could not gain access to the Delta's resources, preserving them rather for the wild animals that lived here. During these severe droughts there were constant demands for the Southern Buffalo Fence to be dropped to allow ranchers access to the Delta's grazing and water, but the government steadfastly refused and for once the fences served the interests of the wildlife.

Before the fences started going up, the Okavango had been protected from the ravages of cattle largely by the presence of tsetse fly. When the tsetse population plunged after the rinderpest epidemic of 1894, the entire region was opened up to cattle farmers: cattle trails and posts spread across the region, especially in areas close to waterways like the Khwai River. Fortunately for the wildlife, the fly population recovered before the cattle had become too entrenched here, and humans and their herds were once again driven to the periphery of the Delta – where, with the help of the fences, they have remained. The isolated tsetse fly populations that exist in the central Delta today no longer protect the wildlife that live here, and the region relies on the veterinary fences that initially so enraged conservationists, for this purpose.

Opposite top: *The downside of ecotourism: a leopard cub plays with a discarded plastic bag.* Opposite bottom: *With extraordinary skill and patience, a helicopter pilot herds buffalo through the Northern Buffalo Fence.* Right: *One of the endless lines of veterinary cordon fencing that divide Botswana's wilderness.*

With the recent completion of the Northern Buffalo Fence, however, conservationists are once again crying foul. Few, if any, were consulted and although the alignment of the fence has been changed, it remains an impenetrable barrier to migrating animals. Seasonal migrations between the Delta and the Caprivi Strip to the north are now virtually impossible, and will become even more difficult with the completion of the electrified fence on the southern edge of the Caprivi. Movement of buffalo, elephant and antelope through here has now effectively been halted and the area between the two fences has been opened up as potential cattle rangeland. The effect of these fences on the region's wildlife populations has yet to be seen, but now that traditional migration routes between dry-season and wet-season grazing areas are effectively cut off, it is inevitable that there will be losses both within and outside of the fences. On the other hand, predictions of a die-off of the entire region's wildlife are probably overly alarmist, bearing in mind that the region's animals have had to deal with the constantly changing natural Okavango environment, with its shifts of water distribution and grazing, since time immemorial.

Although the erection of these new fences has certainly led to the loss of large tracts of wilderness, they may turn out to be the Delta's saving grace, protecting the pristine areas within their embrace from the harmful elements that are gathering on the periphery. Before the Northern Buffalo Fence was finally closed, the DWNP supervised the herding of buffalo by helicopter into the protected fenced area. It seems that this kind of action will, in the end, only be for the benefit of the wildlife. With the erection of the fences, roads to the area have been improved, giving greater access to poachers; one can only hope that this relatively new threat will

The future of the Okavango is inextricably linked with that of the country's cattle industry.

be countered by the protection now offered by the reserves. The Department of Animal Health and Production has recently agreed to work with the DWNP and interested conservation agencies to develop animal-friendly fences that would control the access of cattle to the area but still allow the passage of wildlife.

In effect the fences create a protected wilderness area far larger than the one formally in existence. Together with the Moremi Game Reserve, the Chobe National Park to its northeast, and the buffer zones of the peripheral wildlife management areas and communal hunting areas, the Okavango is one of the largest wildernesses left in the world today. With the enclosing fences, it is also probably one of the more secure.

Recent developments have led to the construction of more fences. In the mid-1990s Botswana's Ngamiland herd was afflicted with contagious bovine pleural pneumonia, apparently after coming into contact with infected animals from Namibia. In a desperate attempt to control the spread of the disease the government erected three new fences stretching west from the Delta to the Namibian border. The construction of the fences ultimately failed in its aim and the entire Ngamiland herd of more than 300 000 head of cattle was destroyed. Ranchers were paid out a proportion of their losses in cash and the remainder with disease-free cattle, to be distributed when the disease was finally under control. Restocking efforts have recently begun.

Beyond the fences and national boundaries, however, lie further threats. Botswana's neighbours covet the precious commodity of water which the Okavango River carries through Namibia on its journey to the Delta. At the best of times a dry country with few water resources of its own, Namibia suffered a severe drought for half of the 1990s, which eventually reached crisis proportions. Facing pressure to provide its capital, Windhoek, with water, the Namibian government has been forced to consider its options. The Okavango River is a tempting source

of water which could feed the capital in a cost-effective way, and although there has been considerable local outcry, Namibia has few alternatives. Desalinisation plants and pipelines to carry water from the coast are simply not financially viable options.

Namibia's plans at this stage are to construct a pipeline to carry water from the Okavango River to the Grootfontein pipeline, and so provide Windhoek with the balance of its water requirements. Opinions regarding the effect that this water capture will have vary widely. Initial reaction verged on the panic-stricken, with speculations of the Okavango Delta drying up within a year. Others reckon that if done at the right time of year, and at a sustainable rate, the pumping will have little effect on the region's wildlife, which is already used to considerable local shifts in water distribution. As worrying is the impact that the implementation of these proposals may have on the subsistence farmers living on the Delta's periphery, and the consequent effects on the Delta. Such an impact, felt at a socio-economic level by the region's poorer inhabitants, could only be counterbalanced by these farmers being given greater access to the Delta's resources.

Already those who use the Delta's resources, mostly within the Panhandle, have made their presence felt. The people who live here have traditionally exploited the river's fish resources at little more than a subsistence level. Recently, in an attempt to raise the region's economic status, international aid organisations have given fishermen in the area access to more effective fishing methods, including motorised fishing craft, gill nets and commercial freezers. The uncontrolled use of this technology has, according to many who know the area intimately, had a noticeable impact on the regional environment. Some channels are severely overfished – one channel reportedly had 42 nets laid along a single kilometre-long stretch. Nearby islands have become increasingly littered with fishing tackle, and some islands, traditionally used as stopovers on tourist *mokoro* trips, are rapidly

losing their appeal. Local recreational anglers have also noticed a severe drop-off in the numbers of fish taken, compared with the catches of a few years ago.

Even the making of *mekoro* (considered by many to be the quintessential Okavango image) and the much-admired local basketware have had a marked effect on the environment. With the demand for the intricately woven baskets increasing, more and more real fan palm fronds are being removed on an unsustainable basis. In some areas the palms have experienced a considerable local decline, but while these are rather isolated cases and not likely to threaten the palm's existence in the region as a whole, they are another example of the unchecked utilisation of resources that could be an indicator of future trends if allowed to continue.

Mokoro-building has led to considerable demand for jackalberries, sausage trees and mangosteens, the trees traditionally used to make the dugout craft. In some areas the most sought-after trees are simply no longer available in suitable sizes. Some *mekoro* we saw were so small, or made from such heavy, unsuitable woods, that they were obviously unusable. A local entrepreneur has developed fibreglass *mekoro* that are apparently now in great demand by local polers and lodges in the area. In a promising new development a major vehicle finance company has agreed to provide assistance to polers wishing to acquire these new craft.

Ultimately, however, the tourists that create the demand for the baskets and *mekoro* have a crucial say in the lasting protection of the Delta. For the last few decades, the cattle and tourism industries have lived side by side as Botswana's highest incomeearners after diamonds. Recently, however, the tourism market has boomed, with the vast majority of visitors flocking to Botswana's spectacular wildlife resources. Foreign exchange returns from tourism are now higher than those from beef exports – some say as much as four times higher – a startling fact bearing in mind that the tourism industry uses much less land

Above: *A couple of buffalo reach the limit of their route at the Northern Buffalo Fence.* Below: *The Ikoga fence, west of the Delta, where it bisects the main road. Contagious bovine pleural pneumonia and the methods used to control it wiped out 300 000 head of cattle.* Opposite: *A fisherman removes a tiger fish from one of his gill nets. This method of fishing has had a serious impact on fish populations in the Okavango.*

than the beef industry and is currently operating at only partial occupancy. In 1995 tourism provided around 27 000 formal and informal jobs, a figure that continues to grow annually. Visitors to the northern national parks doubled between 1994 and 1995, and during the year I spent in the Okavango working on this project there was a noticeable increase in the number of self-drive visitors.

A negative side-effect of the tourism boom is the increase in traffic, both airborne and waterborne. The constant hopping from Maun to lodge and back by charter aircraft has made this town's airport one of the busiest in southern Africa, and the drone of light aircraft passing overhead is an all too common sound, disturbing the peace of the wilderness. On the region's waterways, noise and pollution by local and tourist traffic has led to some concession-holders banning the use of motorboats within their areas.

Despite the considerable political backing still enjoyed by the cattle industry, the local populace is beginning to stand up for its wildlife heritage. A large proportion of the area's residents rely on the lucrative ecotourism industry for employment, and the decline in numbers of many species has come to their attention. As a direct response, the Okavango People's Wildlife Trust (OPWT) was formed and its first conference held in 1997. Realising the potential consequences of the various threats confronting the Delta, the conference took a hard-line stand against them all.

One of the industries targeted was commercial hunting. For some time reports have suggested that the size of commercial hunting trophies taken has been on the decline, with some unethical operators reportedly taking sub-adult animals. Efforts to educate hunting operators in the sustainable management of their concessions have begun, and the number of trophies taken has dropped. Nonetheless, the OPWT conference called for a ban on all hunting within the Okavango, apart from subsistence hunting and the destruction of problem animals (those that destroy crops or eat livestock). The latter is a controversial matter in its own right, and one which is made only slightly less so by the requirement that people have a permit to hunt such animals. The conference further called for existing hunting concessions to be converted to use for photographic safaris.

In responding to its citizens' demands on environmental issues, the Botswanan government has quite a reasonable track record. When proposals were made for the dredging of the Boro River in the southern Delta in 1990, the local residents objected to the plan and pleas were made for the Delta's protection at a *kgotla* (town meeting) in Maun. The government first suspended and later terminated the project. If the momentum behind the OPWT continues, it is probable that the people of Ngamiland will be able to save the Okavango from further degradation.

When considering the many threats the Delta faces, it is all too easy to lose sight of the fact that it is still one of the world's most pristine wilderness areas. The DWNP's policy of high-cost, low-volume tourism has left the Delta, and particularly Moremi Game Reserve, one of the least crowded wildlife reserves on the African continent. Although Moremi is among Botswana's most visited attractions, it is still possible to explore its splendour for an entire day without coming across another vehicle, something which is seldom possible in the continent's other sanctuaries.

While not envying the difficult decisions that lie in the hands of the country's officials, I hope that the visual testament to the Okavango's wilderness contained in these pages serves to inspire them to strive for the Delta's continued protection. I hope, further, that this book does not eventually serve as an epitaph.

The best time to visit the Okavango Delta is between April and October, when animals gather around permanent water during the dry season. November to March is the main rainy season and some lodges close at this time. Roads can be treacherous, sometimes impassable, and the game moves into the woodlands. The area can be very busy during regional school holidays so it is advisable to book well in advance if you intend visiting at these times.

Maun, the main access point to the Delta, is serviced regularly by flights from Johannesburg, Victoria Falls, Gabarone, Harare, Kasane and Windhoek, and charter aircraft constantly ferry guests to and from the various lodges.

Thanks to a dramatic improvement in the condition of Botswana's roads in the last few years, it is now also possible to reach Maun by car on tarred roads from Namibia, Zimbabwe and South Africa. Getting into the Delta itself is another story. Apart from the western edge of the Delta and Panhandle, which are serviced by a good tar road, you will need a four-wheel-drive vehicle to explore the Delta. If you do not have your own, you can hire one in Maun.

Exploration of the Okavango by yourself is restricted to the Panhandle and the public areas of Moremi Game Reserve. You need to be fully self-sufficient for a journey to Moremi. All roads within the reserve require a four-wheel-drive vehicle, and in the wet season, even that will sometimes not cope with the road conditions. Good local maps, like Veronica Roodt's *The Shell Map of Moremi Game Reserve*, are available, and it is also advisable to enquire locally about road conditions in the reserve before leaving Maun. If there has been heavy rain recently, the roads through the mopane forests to tourist areas may well be water-logged; as the rainy season wears on, the passage of heavy vehicles causes conditions to deteriorate.

Driving conditions vary widely in Moremi, so it is important to have a good understanding of how to drive your vehicle in challenging situations. Mud, water and thick sand are the most common obstacles, and track conditions worsen each time some-one gets stuck. It is unnecessary, indeed inadvisable, to create fresh tracks to avoid difficult road conditions. The area around the obstacle (say, a stretch of thick sand or a puddle), is unlikely to be in better condition than the track itself, and leaving the track only increases your chances of getting stuck. This is particularly important to remember when attempting to cross water or a waterlogged track. Driving blindly into a long stretch of water is a daunting task, but the track itself should be compact from vehicles passing over the years. Soil in the mopane forests is extremely clayey and areas bordering the main track get very sticky when wet; the possibility of being bogged down if you leave the track is thus very high indeed. There is not much traffic on these tracks during the wet season and you could be in for a long wait if you do get stuck! If possible, drive in convoy.

Visitors to the area have made the tracks over decades and they access all the best game-viewing areas; almost every photograph in this book was taken from the main tourist tracks. If you are unlucky and see nothing on these tracks, it is unlikely that you will find anything off them. Furthermore, straying from the path is harmful to the environment and illegal.

Fuel is not available in Moremi Game Reserve so visitors need to carry all their fuel requirements; remember to consider game-drives and difficult road conditions when calculating how much fuel you will need. Lodges in Moremi will not sell fuel to self-drive visitors as they have limited supplies, and having to return to Maun, the nearest place to fill your tanks, to obtain extra fuel is a costly and time-consuming experience.

Maun is becoming an increasingly sophisticated town and provisions for your safari can be purchased there. Several large supermarkets, restaurants, banks, service stations and hotels cater for visitors' needs. Note that the movement of meat and other animal products between districts within Botswana is strictly controlled; permits are needed for this purpose, so it is advisable to buy any meat you will need in Maun.

Public campsites within Moremi Game Reserve need to be booked in advance and anyone arriving at the park entrances without a booking will not be admitted. A deposit is payable upon reservation and the remaining fees (payable only in Pula, the local currency) at the entrance gate. It is helpful to advise the Parks & Reserves Reservations Office if you are not going to take up a booking, as sites are limited.

The campsites in Moremi Game Reserve all have ablution facilities, although the upkeep of some leaves much to be desired. Although it is advisable to take your own bottled drinking water, water for ablutions is provided, and you can enjoy hot water if you light a fire under the boiler. Firewood may be collected within the park, but for the sake of conservation only dead wood should be collected, and that sparingly. There is no electricity in the campsites and the use of generators is prohibited.

When camping in Moremi, bear in mind that it is a wilderness area, where you are a visitor in the animals' territory. Campsites are unfenced, so do not sleep in the open – wild animals have severely injured several people ignoring this advice. Baboon, hyaena and other animals open tents with ease and will not hesitate to devour all food inside, or anything resembling food, such as medicines and toiletries. To prevent this, keep food and medicines in securely locked metal containers or in your vehicle whenever you are not using them, or take them with you if you leave the camp. Anything left lying around – from soap to shoes to pots – may be eaten! Although bins are provided, it is better to take all litter with you when you leave. If you need a toilet while out on a drive, dig a hole at least 40 centimetres deep and burn any toilet paper you use. Offroad driving, night driving, camping in undesignated areas and walking are strictly prohibited within the Game Reserve.

An alternative to exploring the region yourself is to join one of the many mobile safaris that operate in the area. There is a wide range of options available, from participation safaris, where the guest is expected to assist in the day-to-day running of the camp, to luxury safaris which in some instances rival the region's

plushest lodges. In all cases a licensed guide, who will normally have an intimate knowledge of the region, will accompany you.

For those who enjoy their creature comforts when getting back to nature, the Okavango Delta is the ultimate destination. With a host of first-rate lodges spread throughout the Delta's various habitats, the only problem that might be encountered is which to choose. In general, the lodges offer luxury accommodation, excellent cuisine throughout the day and a range of activities that give guests the full Okavango experience. Most lodges have 220V generated electricity and hot water. Depending on the location of the lodge, activities on offer range from game drives, *mokoro* and motorboat trips to game-viewing walks, all of which are accompanied by professional guides. There are several lodges in the Khwai and Xakanaxa areas of Moremi Game Reserve; the rest are situated in private concessions and access is restricted to lodge guests. Apart from those in Moremi, access to and from lodges is by chartered light aircraft from Maun. Most charter flights impose a weight limit on baggage, so it is important to find out beforehand what this is and pack accordingly.

In addition to land- and water-based safaris, game-viewing flights are becoming increasingly popular, the most spectacular being those by helicopter, because of the craft's manoeuvrability.

Although the weather is generally quite pleasant, with average maximum temperatures in winter and summer being 25 °C and 32 °C respectively, temperatures can reach uncomfortable extremes. Nights can be bitterly cold in winter, and it can also be rather chilly during early morning and late evening activities; although most lodges provide blankets during activities, it is best to come prepared. During the day, sun protection should be taken seriously: hats and sunblock are essential, and it is also advisable to wear loose clothing that protects the arms and neck.

The Okavango lies within a malaria area so suitable prophylactics should be taken. Consult your physician beforehand about the most appropriate medication to take.

The local currency is the Pula, made up of 100 thebe. Foreign currency is not accepted for purchases in towns, but you can change money at banks in Maun and most larger towns *en route* to the Delta. Most hotels and lodges will accept major credit cards, foreign exchange and traveller's cheques.

Stomach problems from either tap water in Maun or water from the Delta are rare, although if at all unsure about the status of water visitors should use bottled water. Although self-drive visitors to Botswana should carry a good first aid kit, guides and managers at lodges are generally qualified first aiders.

Contact numbers:

Parks & Reserves Reservations Office
P O Box 20364
Boseja
Maun
Botswana
Tel: (+267) 66-1265
Fax: (+267) 66-1264

Camp Moremi, Camp Okavango and Nxabega
Desert & Delta Safaris
P O Box 1200
Paulshof
2056
South Africa
Tel: (+27) (011) 807-3720
Fax: (+27) (011) 807-3480

Khwai River Lodge and Eagle Island Camp
Gametrackers Botswana
P O Box 2608
Cape Town
8000
South Africa
Tel: (+27) (021) 23-1054
Fax: (+27) (021) 23-1061

Drotsky's Cabins and Makwena Lodge
Jan & Eileen Drotsky
P O Box 115
Shakawe
Botswana
Tel: (+267) 67-5035
Fax: (+267) 67-5043

Tsaro Elephant Lodge and Xugana Lodge
Hartley's Safaris
Private Bag 48
Maun
Botswana
Tel: (+267) 66-1806
Fax: (+267) 66-0528

Xakanaxa Camp
Moremi Safaris
P O Box 2757
Cramerview
2060
South Africa
Tel: (+27) (011) 465-3842
Fax: (+27) (011) 465-3779

Helicopter Charter and Game-Viewing Flights
Wildlife Helicopters
Private Bag 161
Maun
Botswana
Tel/fax: (+267) 660-664

BIBLIOGRAPHY

Albertson, Arthur (1997) 'Botswana: Death by Cattle'. Self-published.

Augustinus, Paul (1997) *Desert Adventure: In Search of Wilderness in Namibia and Botswana*. Acorn Books, Randburg.

Balfour, Daryl (1990) *Okavango: An African Paradise*. Struik, Cape Town.

Balfour, Daryl & Sharna (1997) *African Elephants: A Celebration of Majesty*. Struik, Cape Town.

Botswana Society (1976) *Proceedings of the Symposium on the Okavango Delta and its Future Utilisation*. National Museum, Gabarone.

Butchart, Duncan (1995) *Wild about the Okavango*. Southern Books, Halfway House.

Comley, Peter and Meyer, Salome (1994) *Traveller's Guide to Botswana*. New Holland, London.

Dennis, Nigel and Tarboton, Warwick (1993) *Waterbirds: Birds of Southern Africa's Wetlands*. Struik, Cape Town.

Ellery, William & Karen (1997) *Plants of the Okavango Delta*. Tsaro Publishers, Durban.

Estes, Richard (1993) *The Safari Companion: A Guide to Watching African Mammals*. Russel Friedman Books, Halfway House.

Ginn, Peter, McIlleron, Geoff and Milstein, Peter (eds) (1989) *The Complete Book of Southern African Birds*. Struik Winchester, Cape Town.

Johnson, Peter & Bannister, Anthony (1977) *Okavango: Sea of Land, Land of Water*. Struik, Cape Town.

Joyce, Peter and Balfour, Daryl & Sharna (1994) *This is Botswana*. New Holland, London.

Lanting, Frans (1993) *Okavango: Africa's Last Eden*. Russel Friedman Books, Halfway House.

Lee, Douglas (1990) 'Okavango Delta: Old Africa's Last Refuge'. *National Geographic*, Vol. 178, No. 6.

Lomba, Rick (1992) 'Conservation & development: Botswana's cattle experience' Executive Summary – Okavango Wildlife Society, Parklands.

Main, Michael (1987) *Kalahari: Life's Variety in Dune and Delta*. Southern Books, Halfway House.

McNutt, John *et al.* (1996) *Running Wild: Dispelling the Myths of the African Wild Dog*. Southern Books, Halfway House.

Mills, Gus and Hes, Lex (eds.) (1997) *The Complete Book of Southern African Mammals*. Struik Winchester, Cape Town.

Newman, Kenneth (1983) *Newman's Birds of Southern Africa*. Southern Books, Halfway House.

Okavango Research Group (1996) *Papers published in the period 1986–1990, 1990–1993, 1993–1994 and 1994–1996*. University of the Witwatersrand, Johannesburg.

Pickford, Peter & Beverly and Tarboton, Warwick (1989) *Southern African Birds of Prey*. Struik, Cape Town.

Roodt, Veronica (1993) *The Shell Guide to the Trees of the Okavango Delta and Moremi Game Reserve*. Shell Oil Botswana, Gabarone.

Roodt, Veronica (1996) *The Shell Tourist Guide to Botswana*. Shell Oil Botswana, Gabarone.

Ross, Karen (1987) *Okavango: Jewel of the Kalahari*. BBC Books, London.

Scott, Jonathan (1996) *Dawn to Dusk: A Safari through Africa's Wild Places*. BBC Books, London.

Skinner, John and Smithers, Reay (1990) *The Mammals of the Southern African Subregion* (second edition). University of Pretoria, Pretoria.

Tinley, Ken (1966) *An Ecological Reconnaissance of the Moremi Wildlife Reserve, Northern Okavango Swamps, Botswana*. Okavango Wildlife Society, Johannesburg.

Page numbers in *italics* refer to illustrations